The HONEY COMPANION

The HONEY COMPANION

Natural Recipes and Remedies for Health, Beauty, and Home

SUZY SCHERR

THE COUNTRYMAN PRESS
A division of W. W. Norton & Company
Independent Publishers Since 1923

For information about permission to reproduce selections from this book, write
to Permissions, The Countryman Press, 500 Fifth Avenue, New York, NY 10110

For information about special discounts for bulk purchases, please contact
W. W. Norton Special Sales at specialsales@wwnorton.com or 800-233-4830

Manufacturing by Versa Press
Production manager: Devon Zahn

The Countryman Press
www.countrymanpress.com

A division of W. W. Norton & Company, Inc.
500 Fifth Avenue, New York, NY 10110
www.wwnorton.com

978-1-68268-374-3 (pbk.)

10 9 8 7 6 5 4 3 2 1

To MAS, who is sweeter than honey.

CONTENTS

DRESSINGS, DRIZZLES, SPREADS, AND SAUCES 82

BAKED AND SWEET THINGS 92

PART THREE: Honey for Health 111

PART FOUR: Honey for Beauty 143

PART FIVE: Mind Your Beeswax (Household Uses for Honey and Beeswax) 169

ADDITIONAL RESOURCES 189

PART ONE

GETTING STARTED WITH HONEY

INTRODUCTION

You know bees make honey. And you know honey is delicious. You've probably used it to sweeten tea, maybe drizzled it on a biscuit or some toast here and there, and also . . . well, okay, mostly in tea, right? But I'll let you in on a little secret: Honey is so much more than *just* a sweetener. It is, as a matter of fact, liquid magic—deliciously complex, full of nutritional and medicinal benefits—a real powerhouse with scores of amazing uses both in and out of the kitchen.

Indeed, using honey on the regular will change your life and—thanks to the amazing work of bees—benefit the planet. Sounds like an overstatement, I know, but I assure you it is not. As a working mom with a talent for juggling that is not quite on par with the number of balls I have in the air at any given moment, I love honey for its everyday problem-solving capacity. Honey is my go-to for so many things all over the house that my kids probably think Winnie the Pooh is a not-so-distant relative.

As a chef, I often turn to honey for its unique flavor and texture, both of which transform salad dressings, sauces, savory dishes, desserts, and cocktails—adding depth, complexity, and natural sweetness to dishes of all kinds. Honey can balance strong or acidic flavors like nobody's business. And while the simplicity of a spoonful of honey in (yes) tea is comfort epitomized, there's also a lot of powerful science behind how and why it heals and helps us feel better when we're under the weather. Seriously, how many tasty ingredients can you think of that can heal a wound, ease a sore throat, calm an upset stomach, boost your energy, nourish your body, and give you the complexion of a Hollywood starlet? Not many, I bet—but honey can do all that and more.

Rich in vitamins and minerals, and with antioxidant and antibacterial properties, honey has been shown to soothe ulcers, burns, skin sores, and inflammation. It's an amazing beauty treatment, natural digestive aid, sugar alternative, allergy treatment, energy invigorator, skin salve, and topical antiseptic. And studies have shown that honey does a better job of easing nighttime coughs and improving sleep than do many popular cough suppressants. So . . . take *that*, spoonful of sugar! Better yet, honey is easy to find, easy to use, and keeps—literally— forever, so you can bulk-shop the heck out the stuff and always have enough on hand for whatever you're up to. And to prove it, here's your comprehensive guide to the many diverse and delicious ways you can use honey every day to enhance your life.

In other words, it's all about how honey is the bee's knees.

A Brief History of Honey

Honey has been around for a long time. Like, 100 million years long. It's basically as old as history is itself. Although there are cave paintings in Spain that suggest people have been harvesting it for 8,000 years, give or take, scientists believe that beekeeping as we know it began in earnest in ancient Egypt around 2500 BCE. Since then, honey's magical properties and usefulness have given it a noteworthy place in history, as humans have eaten it, bathed in it, treated their wounds with it, traded it, and even paid their taxes with it (really!).

In ancient Greece and Rome, honey was not just food and medicine, but symbolized fertility, love, and beauty. In Egypt, archaeologists discovered honey that had been buried with other valuables in King Tut's tomb alongside his body; 3,000 years later, the honey was perfectly preserved and completely edible. (Wouldn't you love to know who got to taste it? My money's on the intern.) According to myth, Cupid used to dip his arrows in honey to fill a lover's heart with sweetness. In Greece, even now, it is customary for a bride to dip her finger into honey for a sweet life. Honey is also traditionally eaten on the Jewish New Year, Rosh Hashanah, to bring sweetness and good fortune in the year ahead. And honey's usage in many modern Italian recipes is a vestige of its importance in ancient Rome all those years ago.

Fast-forward to the 1100s and people were eating a lot of freaking honey! This was before sugar came on the scene; it is estimated that Europeans were chowing down on about 4½ pounds of honey per year to satisfy their sweet tooth. When the United States was colonized, settlers actually brought honeybees with them to be used as a free source of sugar. Sometime after World War II, people learned about the importance of honeybees in pollinating crops and began to incorporate uses for honey in modern medicine. Even so, by the turn of the 20th century, honey had finally become eclipsed by sugar. Sugar mills had started to pop up in the 1400s and, although it started out as such a rare commodity that it was considered a fine spice, sugar steadily gained speed and popularity. Over time, honey consumption dropped to less than ½ pound per person per year. Interestingly, however, according to latest data from the United States Department of Agriculture (USDA), honey use has risen again in recent years—perhaps due to better education and shifting taste preferences—with an annual average of nearly 1 pound of honey consumed per person, even as consumption of other caloric sweeteners has been steadily falling. So, long story short—honey has stood the test of time (and time again).

The Busy Life of Bees
What Is Honey and Where Does It Come From?

Inside every beehive is a buzzing, bustling factory where honeybees transform flower nectar into the sweetest elixir on earth. Despite the thousands of honey varieties in the world, the bees' recipe for honey never changes and the organization chart, lines of communication, complex method of nest construction, defense strategy, and division of labor within the hive always stays constant.

First, let's understand who inhabits a beehive. Each colony is made up of three kinds of adult bees: workers, drones, and a queen, each with a clearly defined role within bee civilization.

The thousands of female worker bees are responsible for collecting nectar and pollen, raising the offspring, maintaining optimal hive temperature, gathering food, cleaning house, building the honeycomb, producing wax and royal jelly, defending the hive, serving the queen, and, in all likelihood, driving to soccer practice and making dentist appointments. They don't typically lay eggs because, good gracious, *they can't do everything*! But, they are laser-focused on getting the job done, working from sunrise to sunset. Every. Single. Day. Of their (6-week-long) lives. #girlpower

The few hundred drones (male bees) live in late spring and early summer and are around mainly for the purpose of mating with their queen. They are larger than worker bees, have no stinger, produce no wax, collect no pollen, and must be fed and cared for by the worker bees. Kind of like that high-maintenance dude your roommate dated after college who paid no rent, slept over every night, ate all of your communal food, and—after a few months of sleeping with her—was never seen or heard from again. The difference in the case of bees is that the rest of the colony tolerates drones because their contribution is critical to the survival of the hive.

The ten or so drones that do get a chance to fertilize the queen are in for the surprise of a lifetime when it happens because they die as soon as the deed is done! After he mates with her, the queen rips off the drone's most personal piece of equipment and then he immediately falls to his death. As for the drones that don't get to mate with a queen, come winter . . . they get kicked out. Where do they go? Well, for the most part they just sort of hang around, pathetically hoping they'll be invited back into the hive. But, nope. They don't get to come back in and, eventually, they die. Boy, bye!

Although there is only one queen in a colony of bees that may number as many as 60,000 or more, she is fundamental to

everything that happens within a healthy hive. She is, unsurprisingly, the largest bee in the colony and the star of the kingdom, because of her exclusive ability to lay eggs. How many eggs? She will produce about 1,500 to 2,000 a day. *A day.* That's about one egg every 20 to 30 seconds!

In her lifetime, a queen bee will produce more than her own body weight in eggs. That's effectively a lifetime of permanent PMS, which is why it's completely reasonable that she lives a fairly indulgent lifestyle. When she is one week old, the queen will leave the hive, take several flights to mate with 10 to 20 drones, then come home to lay her eggs, binge-watch old episodes of *Full House*, and never, ever leave the house again. Can you blame her?

After one season of mating, she has enough sperm inside her to continue to fertilize for the rest of her life! And while she's busy makin' babies, thanks to the amazing cooperation and democracy within bee society, the other bees tend to her every need because she physically cannot take care of herself. Her role is to move from cell to cell, laying all those eggs. So, her tireless attendants feed her, groom her, carry away her waste, and even digest her food for her. (*Yeah, I know!* A queen does not have the anatomy to digest her food, which is why it is predigested and then fed to her.) Although laying eggs is her main gig, she also produces chemicals that guide the behavior of the other bees. These chemicals are called pheromones, and they're crucial to keeping the business of bee life on track.

So, then, how *do* bees make honey? Well, it all goes back to those busy worker bees that fly for miles and miles to collect nectar from 100 to 150 flowering plants. They suck the nectar out of flowers with their crazy-long tubular tongue and store it in a special honey stomach (different from their food stomach). When they have a full load, they fly back to the hive, where they pass on the nectar through their mouth to processor worker bees who gnaw on it for about half an hour, adding an enzyme called invertase that breaks down the sucrose portion of the nectar. Then, they pass it on to another processor, who in turn passes it on again.

It's passed around and around, until it eventually becomes a very wet, sweet substance (it's about 70% water), at which point it is stored in the little hexagonal wax cells of the honeycomb—like teensy little honey pots! Since the honey is still quite watery, the bees fan it with their wings to help it dry out and become a sticky substance containing about 18 percent water. Once the nectar has ripened into honey, the processor bees "cap" the cell with an airtight wax seal made from wax flakes they excrete from their abdomen—and presto! The honey is ready for bees to feed on all year round—and fortunately for us, they usually make more than they need, so we can have some, too.

Sweet fact: It takes at least eight bees all their life to make one single teaspoonful of honey.

The Importance of Honeybees and How to Keep Them Safe

Bees and all that they symbolize have been long loved through the ages, depicted and celebrated in art, song, ceremony, poetry, spirituality, structural design, and philosophy, because we humans figured out early on about the big, important contribution bees make to our world. Sure, they produce glorious, golden honey, which is awesome and all, but in the process of doing that they contribute something even more unbelievably beneficial for humanity and the environment—they *pollinate*! Why is this so important? Well, because without pollination, nothing would grow and we'd have no fruits, vegetables, berries, nuts, leaves, roots, or seeds. And if you think *that* sounds like a big problem, consider the fact that farmers rely on honeybees to pollinate many of the crops that feed their livestock—

without bees to pollinate such plants as clover and alfalfa, we'd have no meat, eggs, cheese, or milk. Even coffee is pollinated by bees.

So you see, honeybees (and wild bees) play a pretty pivotal role in the whole food chain. And the contribution of bees reaches even further than food and flowers. Bees also pollinate many trees, which support wildlife, help even out soil composition and landscapes, and are our planet's lungs. So, yeah, you could say they're important.

Now, I have good news and bad news. I'll quickly get the bad news over with so we can get back to the Yay-for-the-Bees party: Bees are in trouble. Climate change, habitat loss, pesticides, and disease are wreaking havoc with them. Every year in the United States, colonies lose an average of 30 to 40 percent

of their population. Talk about a buzzkill (sorry—couldn't help myself). The good news: There are things you can do to help make our world a great place for honeybees and other wild pollinators—and you don't necessarily have to become a beekeeper (though you *could*!). Here are the top five ways you can help save the bees:

1. Plant a bee-friendly garden. Native plants provide great sources of nectar and pollen (both food for the bees and butterflies). And while you're at it, ditch weeding (tell the truth: you didn't want to weed your garden anyway, did you?). Many plants—dandelion, for example—are an excellent source of food for bees. In early spring, those "weeds" are often the only source of food for beneficial insects. (See more tips concerning this on page 192.)

2. Don't use pesticides, fungicides, or herbicides on plants. They become contaminated with the chemicals, which will likely reach the bees and kill them.

3. Put out a water source for the bees. A shallow birdbath or even a dish near your flowering plants will do the trick. Just be sure to put a few stones or floating cork on the water, so the bees won't drown!

4. Learn how to become a beekeeper or adopt a hive! Of course, you could dive in headfirst and install a hive in your garden or on your rooftop and become a legit backyard beekeeper. But if you're not yet up to the challenge of keeping bees and want to do something to keep these amazing creatures safe, you can always "adopt" a hive. Many local beekeepers or national associations, for an annual fee, will allow you to support the work of beekeepers. By doing so, you'll get honey and other products from your adopted hive, along with information and other fun stuff. You may even have the opportunity to visit your bees!

5. Eat more honey! Support beekeepers—by buying their local and raw honey.

All of Your Beeswax: Royal Jelly, Bee Pollen, Beeswax, and Other Products from the Hive

Beeswax. When bees reach a certain age, they naturally produce wax flakes through a complex digestive process in glands located on the underside of their abdomen. They use the wax to build the hexagonal cells of the beehive (the honeycomb) in which they raise their offspring and store honey. When harvested from a hive, humans can utilize beeswax in lots of cool ways.

Many cosmetic products, such as facial creams, masks, lotions, and lipsticks, use beeswax as an ingredient. (Hi, Burt!) Candles made from beeswax burn cleaner, releasing less carcinogenic soot, and look beautiful. And beeswax is a key ingredient in pharmaceutical and dental products, floor and furniture polish, crayons, candy, chewing gum, ski wax, and tons of other well-known products—helping each to be firm yet pliable, hydrating, softening, protecting, and/or lubricating.

As you'll see later in the book, beeswax is indispensable around the house. From crafting to home remedies to creating all-natural, greener alternatives to otherwise *un*natural products that we use every day, beeswax is fun and easy to work with. When buying beeswax, you may notice that it comes in a variety of colors and forms—yellow, white, block, pellet . . . Color variation has to do with how much the wax has been filtered and/or how much time it spent in the hive. White wax, for example, has had all of its pollen removed, whereas dark yellow wax has hung out in the hive for a good while. You can buy beeswax from a local bee farmer, but it's also readily available online. Bags of beeswax pellets are great for projects that involve melting the wax; solid bars work best for instances where you'd want to rub the wax on a surface.

Bee pollen. File this under "More Amazing Things Bees Can Do": In addition to collecting nectar from flowers, honeybees fly from plant to plant gathering sticky pollen in "baskets" on their legs, which they later mix with saliva and nectar and pack into tidy little pellets that are stored in honeycomb cells. These little pollen nuggets become a highly nutritious food source for worker bees and larvae. Some science suggests that bee pollen may be beneficial to humans, because it is rich in amino acids and high in vitamins. Bee pollen is believed to accelerate healing, revitalize the body, and protect cells from free radicals, which is why you're so likely to see it on the list of add-ins at your local smoothie bar.

Propolis. Also known as "bee glue," propolis is an incredibly sticky, gummy substance that worker bees gather from trees and plants. It's basically a cocktail of resin, sap, balm, wax, essential oils, pollen, and minerals that bees use as cement when building the hive. They use it to plug holes, stabilize moveable parts, shellac interior walls, and defend against extreme weather and intruders. Propolis is believed to be rich in many vitamins and other nutrients that make it an antibacterial, antiviral, antifungal, antibiotic, anti-inflammatory, and antioxidant. Many people take it as a supplement to relieve joint pain, treat eczema, alleviate gastrointestinal discomfort, and stimulate the immune system.

Royal jelly. Some worker bees called nurse bees produce a creamy, white substance—royal jelly—that they secrete from glands near their head region and feed to newborn bees for the first few days of their life. Sounds like royal jelly is some kind of supercharged baby food, used to get little bees off on the right foot, right? Yes. Except it's more than that, because royal jelly is also responsible for transforming a common bee into a queen, extending her prolonged existence from six weeks to five years. So, it's queen food, too.

Worker bees begin the process of "growing" a new queen by filling a special cell in the comb with royal jelly. The larva selected to be the future queen spends her early days literally *swimming* in the stuff, ultimately transforming her genetic makeup into that of a queen, who will be fed royal jelly for the rest of her life.

The chemical makeup of royal jelly bewilders scientists because of its highly complex compounds, but is known to have antibacterial, antiviral, antibiotic, energizing, nutritive, and antiaging properties. Full of B vitamins and vitamins A, E, and C, enzymes, fatty acids, sterols, gelatin, and immunizing proteins (to defend bees against infection) royal jelly is purported to lower blood pressure and cholesterol levels; to improve fertility, relieve menopausal symptoms, and prevent osteoporosis; and to significantly eliminate the free radicals that normally cause premature cell aging. It is often added to cosmetics but may also be taken at home as a supplement, sold at health food stores in capsule, powder, or fresh-frozen form.

Selecting, Buying, and Storing Honey

Thanks to honey's trendiness, gourmet shops, farmers' markets, and even our local grocery stores are brimming with fancy flavors and unique varieties of honey. Some are local. Some are raw. Some are foraged from wildflower, clover, buckwheat, orange blossom, or eucalyptus blossoms. There is light, dark, filtered, and unfiltered honey, some with the honeycomb, and some without. There's honey that is creamed, infused with herbs, and organic, or not. And, believe it or not, a whole lot of honey out there is *fake*! Yep, counterfeit honey is actually a thing and it involves an estimated 76 percent of honey sold in American supermarkets. And there's tainted honey, too, which is also a big problem. Much of our mass-produced honey—often imported from China and India—has a history of contamination, which means that, at best, it's been blended with corn syrup and/or other sweeteners to make it more affordable and, at worst, it's tainted with lead (from soil that's been polluted with heavy metals), antibiotics, and other freaky chemicals that you don't want to know about. Unfortunately, labeling regulations for honey are confusing and get particularly murky when

imported honey gets repackaged, then sold somewhere else. In the United States, the FDA is working on it, but for the time being, labeling regulations just aren't strict or reliable enough to let you know what you're getting or even where it's come from.

So . . . suffice it to say, the large selection of honey out there can be overwhelming and the ambiguous labeling can be nerve-racking, so buying it can actually be kind of a confusing undertaking. In an attempt to demystify the whole nine yards and ensure you're getting the good stuff, here are a few good rules of thumb to keep in mind when shopping for honey.

Choose Local

The best place to shop for honey is locally. That way you know exactly where the honey comes from, and you'll be sure to get the purest product possible. It's always best to buy directly from a local beekeeper, but if your closest honey farmer is too far out of reach, seek out farmers' markets, natural food stores, or a reputable neighborhood grocer who stocks local honey. In other words, try to buy as directly as you can, with as few middlemen or middlewomen as possible.

Buy Raw, Unfiltered Honey

Unless you're cooking or baking with honey, you should pretty much always be using the raw stuff. Why? Because the process of pasteurizing and/or filtering honey (i.e., heating it) not only destroys many of its natural antioxidants, minerals, and enzymes, it strips and changes the honey's nuanced flavor. For the best-tasting honey with the densest nutrition profile, opt for honey that has never been heated over natural hive temperatures, which is about 100°F. Unfortunately, since honey labeling is so thorny, you can't necessarily trust a label, even if it says "100% raw honey." The best way to guarantee that your honey is actually raw is to shop directly from local sources you can trust and ask them about their product. Chances are, they'll be very happy to tell you about it.

Don't Bother Trying to Find Organic Honey

You can skip the organic and GMO-free labels. For honey to be labeled "organic," according to the USDA, it must come from hives that are free of chemicals or located far away from any present. Also, the flowers that the bees get nectar and pollen from cannot be sprayed with chemicals and the bees cannot be given antibiotics. So, yeah, *all* the flowers and the entire foraging area need to be pesticide-free. When you consider the fact that a bee can visit as many as 100 flowers and cover a couple of miles in one trip from the hive, you start to understand how tricky it would be to prove that they weren't exposed to pesticides or antibiotics. Even if the beekeepers *are* doing their part to keep the hive organic, the foraging area is way too large to control in that way, so "organic" on a label is kind of meaningless.

Shop for Flavor

Enough already with the regulations and the warnings! We're not talking about buying an insurance policy here! This is honey for goodness' sake, so first and foremost, you should make sure it tastes delicious. How will you know if it's delicious? Taste it, silly! More than 300 different kinds of honey are produced in the United States—some floral, some citrusy, some mild, and some complex . . . it all depends on the nectar of the flowers the bees visited. These could include orange blossom, lavender, clover, sunflower, buckwheat, or a mixture of wildflowers, to name but a *very* few. With all that variety, you're sure to find something you love.

Tasting honey can get pretty intricate—just as it is for wine, chocolate, and olive oil. Once you get into honey tasting, you might like trying different varietals with a flavor and aroma wheel in hand.

How to Store Honey

This part is pretty straightforward—simply store your honey in a tightly sealed container in a cool place away from direct heat or sunlight. Honey doesn't need to be refrigerated. In fact, you'll find it much harder to deal with if you refrigerate it, so just don't. While honey doesn't ever "go bad," you will notice

MANUKA HONEY: WHAT'S ALL THE BUZZ ABOUT?

Manuka honey is made by bees that pollinate the manuka bush in New Zealand. It has a strong, slightly bitter flavor and was used medicinally in New Zealand for ages before being marketed to the rest of the world. What sets it apart from other honey is its high levels of certain antibacterial compounds, including methylglyoxal (MGO) and leptosperin, which supercharge its potency. Laboratory studies have shown manuka honey may not only kill antibiotic-resistant germs, such as *Staphylococcus aureus* and MRSA, but that it can also be effective in treating infected wounds, burns, and eczema.

that store-bought honey usually has a best-by date printed on the package. This is simply because, over time, honey can sometimes change color and/or crystallize, especially if it's raw. If this happens, warm it up briefly with gentle heat (stick the jar in a bowl of hot tap water or zap it in the microwave for a few seconds) and I promise you, it will beehive—I mean behave.

A warning about babies and honey: Since honey is a natural food, you'd think it would be an ideal choice when it comes to feeding babies and it is, but *only* if they're over 12 months old. Honey can contain spores of a bacterium called *Clostridium botulinum*, which is harmless to older kids and adults, but can germinate in a baby's immature digestive system and cause infant botulism, a rare but potentially fatal illness.

A note for diabetics: Wondering whether honey is a good sugar substitute in a diabetic low-sugar eating plan? In short: not really. Both honey and sugar will impact blood sugar levels. Although honey is sweeter than granulated sugar, and therefore you might use a lot less of it, honey actually has more carbohydrates and more calories per teaspoon than sugar. So, any calories and carbohydrates you save by cutting back will be fairly minimal. In other words, strictly from a carb perspective, there's no real advantage to using honey instead of sugar.

PART TWO

HONEY TO EAT

APPETIZERS, SNACKS, AND SIPS

WHIPPED GOAT CHEESE CROSTINI WITH TRUFFLE HONEY AND THYME

This is definitely one of those whole-is-greater-than-the-sum-of-its-parts kinds of foods. These crostini are so simple, it's almost absurd, yet they are deliciously complex and quite fancy. There's something about the combination of creamy, tangy cheese plus earthy, sweet honey along with a bright, herbal hit of thyme that makes people go absolutely bananas for these. Serve them at your next party and you'll see. I'm serious.

Truffle honey, which is available at gourmet shops and well-stocked supermarkets, is a tad pricey, but a little goes a long way, so a small jar will last you a while. Piping the whipped cheese out of a pastry bag fitted with a large star tip makes for a pretty presentation, but you can always spread the mixture onto the toasts with a short knife before garnishing with thyme and drizzling with honey.

Makes about 24 pieces

1 baguette, cut into ¼-inch slices

1 tablespoon extra-virgin olive oil, or more as needed

Kosher salt

4 ounces soft, mild chèvre-style goat cheese

2 tablespoons heavy whipping cream

1 to 2 tablespoons truffle honey

Fresh thyme leaves for garnish

Continued

1. Preheat the oven to 400°F. Place the baguette slices on a baking sheet. Lightly brush each slice with the olive oil. Sprinkle with salt and bake until lightly toasted and crisp, about 8 minutes. Remove from the oven and allow to cool.

2. Meanwhile, combine the goat cheese and cream in the bowl of a stand mixer fitted with the whisk attachment, or in a medium bowl and reach for your handheld electric mixer. Beat until light, fluffy, and smooth, 1 to 2 minutes.

3. To assemble the crostini, place the whipped goat cheese mixture in a piping bag fitted with a large star tip. Squeeze the mixture onto the baguette slices. Drizzle with the truffle honey and garnish with just a few fresh thyme leaves.

Note: The toasts can be made up to a day ahead and stored in an airtight container.

MISO-HONEY CHICKEN WINGS

Let's face it, really good chicken wings—the kind you can't stop eating, the kind you immediately think of when someone says "game day snacks" or "party food"—aren't really about the chicken at all. I mean, sure, the chicken is good, especially if it's got crispy skin—but what separates just-okay wings from great wings is the sauce. That's the genius of these wings—you get tons of flavor from the sauce in each and every bite. Here, salty, savory miso is beautifully balanced by sweet, floral honey. Plus, you can pull this crazy-simple dish together in just a few minutes with *so few* ingredients.

Serves 4 to 6

⅔ cup honey
⅓ cup mellow white miso
Freshly ground black pepper
Canola, safflower, or another neutral cooking oil for pans
3 pounds whole chicken wings (about 32), patted dry
Kosher salt
Sesame seeds and chopped scallions for garnish

1. Preheat the oven to 450°F.

2. Make the miso-honey glaze: combine the honey and miso in a small bowl and season with the pepper. Set aside.

3. Lightly oil two baking sheets and divide the wings evenly between the pans. Season with salt and pepper and bake

for 30 to 40 minutes, flipping the wings halfway through, until golden brown.

4. Brush the wings with the glaze and bake for 3 minutes more. Remove from the oven, brush with more glaze, sprinkle with sesame seeds and scallions, and serve.

BEWITCHING FIG AND BLUE CHEESE FLATBREAD WITH HONEY AND THYME

I used to love to watch *Bewitched*. Of all the many dilemmas Samantha Stevens would solve with magic, my favorite was watching her deal with unexpected dinner guests. Darrin, her ad exec husband, would regularly spring last-minute additions on her—usually a new client or his boss, Larry Tate. Somehow, even as a kid, I found that predicament to be both thrilling and amusing, which is why I still love to think up ways in which I might save the day (perhaps my husband's) with a dazzling dish that almost magically materializes in an instant.

This recipe, which uses store-bought flatbread (I especially like using naan, which is available in most well-stocked supermarkets or, of course, at your local Indian restaurant), is all at once beautiful to look at, quick to assemble, and Darrin delicious—ahem, darned delicious. While fresh figs are gorgeous, they're also a fabulous textural and flavorful counterpart to the salty, funky blue cheese and a beautiful complement to the honey. Figs' season is short and those of us who don't actually have magic powers may not be able to find them year-round, but that's okay! Peaches, apples, ripe pears, apricots, even dried figs are totally acceptable stand-ins.

Serves 4

1 store-bought flatbread

1 tablespoon olive oil

4 ounces blue cheese, crumbled

4 or 5 fresh figs, thinly sliced

1 teaspoon fresh thyme

Freshly ground black pepper

1 tablespoon honey

1. Preheat the oven to 450°F.

2. Place the flatbread on a pizza pan or baking sheet and brush with the olive oil. Sprinkle evenly with the blue cheese and top with the fig slices. Sprinkle with the thyme and pepper.

3. Bake for 10 minutes, or until the cheese is melted and the flatbread is crisp around the edges. Remove from the oven and drizzle with the honey.

HONEY-GLAZED ALMONDS

A warning: these glazed almonds are totally addictive. I'm just saying. Sweet, salty, crunchy . . . all boxes: check, check, check. They are the perfect nibble with a cocktail, round out a cheese and fruit board with style, and make for quite a lovely hostess gift if you're not the one throwing the party. They're also ridiculously easy to make. As in, mix almonds with honey and salt. Bake. Done. So, consider doubling or even tripling this recipe because you're going to want to keep these nuts around for all kinds of reasons: stirring into yogurt, topping salads, filling lunch boxes, and, of course, straight-up snacking.

Makes 2 cups

3 tablespoons raw honey

2 cups raw almonds

1 teaspoon kosher or coarse sea salt

1. Preheat the oven to 350°F.

2. Warm the honey to liquefy it.

3. Combine the honey and almonds in a large bowl, mixing thoroughly so that all the almonds are coated.

4. Spread the almond mixture on a parchment-lined baking pan and sprinkle evenly with the salt.

5. Bake for 15 to 25 minutes, stirring occasionally, until the nuts are fragrant and toasted.

HONEY-SESAME POPCORN

We are big movie watchers in our house. My husband is the screenings curator and I am in charge of movie snacks. In addition to our love of movies (or because of it?), we are also a household of popcorn lovers, so that's where I usually head when rounding up a snack for everyone's viewing pleasure. While traditional butter and salt can't be beat, I do like to liven things up from time to time with some kind of fun or unexpected topping. This popcorn recipe hits all the notes: crunchy, chewy, sweet, salty. It's a clear-cut crowd-pleaser. And if you like to add spicy to your list of perfect-snack-must-haves, you can always swap out some of the cinnamon for a bit of cayenne or smoked paprika. Now you're movie-ready!

Makes about 6 cups

6 cups popped popcorn

⅓ cup honey

3 tablespoons tahini

1½ teaspoons vanilla extract

¼ teaspoon fine sea salt, plus more for sprinkling

¼ teaspoon ground cinnamon, plus more for sprinkling

2 tablespoons sesame seeds

1. Preheat the oven to 350°F. Line a rimmed baking sheet with parchment paper. Place the popcorn in a large bowl.

2. Place the honey in a small, heavy-bottomed saucepan and bring to a boil over medium heat. Continue to boil for

about 90 seconds, adjusting the heat as necessary so that the syrup doesn't boil over. Remove the pot from the heat.

3. Carefully stir in the tahini, vanilla, salt, and cinnamon. Whisk until well blended, then drizzle over the popcorn. Gently toss with a rubber spatula or big spoon until thoroughly combined. Pour the popcorn onto the prepared baking sheet and arrange it in a single layer. Sprinkle with an even layer of the sesame seeds.

4. Bake the popcorn for 6 minutes, then rotate the pan and bake for another 2 minutes. Remove from the oven and sprinkle with additional cinnamon and salt to taste. The popcorn will continue to crisp as it cools. Once it's cool, break the popcorn into pieces (or leave in chunks) and press Play!

5. Store in an airtight container for up to 3 days.

Note: This recipe tastes best with freshly popped corn, which is easy to make even without an electric popcorn popper. Simply place ⅓ cup of unpopped popcorn kernels in a brown paper lunch bag, fold over the top to close it, and microwave on HIGH for 2½ minutes.

THE BEE'S KNEES COCKTAIL

The Bee's Knees is a classic drink that has stood the test of time. Made of honey syrup and fresh lemon, it's a Prohibition-era cocktail that, like many libations of the day, probably came about as a way to help mask the harshness of all that homemade hooch people were brewing in their bathtub (yes, seriously). This recipe is quick and easy—made with just three simple ingredients, it's perfectly light, refreshing, sweet, and crisp. It's delicious and definitely happy hour–worthy as is, but if you're thinking about how to go next level with this classic concoction, now would be as good a time as any to test out one of those infused honeys you've been wanting to take for a spin. Try something herbal or floral, such as thyme, ginger, rosemary, lavender, or even elderflower—then play around and tweak to your liking. One last note: please, please, please—no bottled lemon juice for this one. Freshly squeezed makes all the difference in the world. Cheers!

Serves 2

3 tablespoons honey

2 tablespoons hot water

½ cup gin

4 tablespoons fresh lemon juice

2 sprigs fresh thyme for garnish (optional)

1. Place the honey in a small bowl. Add the hot water and stir until you achieve a thin syrup. Add the gin and lemon juice.

2. Fill a cocktail shaker with ice.

3. Add the gin mixture; shake well.

4. Strain into two glasses and garnish with thyme, if using.

Chill out: A perfectly chilled glass can keep cocktails colder longer. For a quick chill, fill a glass with crushed ice and a splash of water. Let sit for a few minutes, dump out the ice water, and strain your drink into the glass.

THE QUEEN BEE

My friend and real-life queen bee, Claire Marin, introduced a version of this recipe to me not long ago. *Okay, fine, she isn't* actually *a bee!* But she *is* an amazing beekeeper and entrepreneur, who tends over 300 hives in New York State, sells an incredible line of artisanal foods utilizing local natural resources (some of which are on the menus of New York City's top restaurants), and is the maker of a truly unique honey-infused whiskey. What's cooler is that she's one of only about 9 or 10 female distillers in an industry of over 1,700 men! Q-U-E-E-N! Claire's original recipe for this drink, of course, incorporates her very own NY Honey Rye. You can (and should!) use that in this recipe if you happen to be lucky enough to get your hands on some, but if you want to DIY it with something you already have in your liquor cabinet, here's an adaptation that is delicious and similarly honey-ish without being overly sweet. It's bright, intense, and a little bit spicy—a flavor note that is enhanced by honey, which offers nuance that sugar's one-note sweetness can't. This is a great recipe for using any intense, bold honey you have in your cabinet, such as chestnut or buckwheat, but any varietal will work just fine. For a truly custom cocktail, try infusing the honey syrup with herbs, spices, or citrus peel. Then, toast to all the badass women out there (like Claire) who are *bustin' it* to make the world a better, more delicious place.

Serves 2

2 tablespoons honey

1 tablespoon boiling water

½ cup rye whiskey

2 tablespoons ginger liqueur

2 tablespoons fresh lemon juice

2 lemon twists for garnish

1. Pour the honey into a small bowl. Add the hot water and stir until you achieve a thin syrup.

2. Add the rye, ginger liqueur, and lemon juice to the honey syrup.

3. Fill a cocktail shaker with ice.

4. Add the rye mixture; shake well.

5. Strain into two glasses and garnish with lemon twists.

ENDLESSLY CUSTOMIZABLE HONEY SYRUP FOR HOMEMADE SODA

This honey syrup and its gazillion variations are great to have on hand for adding quick flavor and a touch of sweetness to all kinds of beverages. With nothing other than honey, fruit, herbs, and spices—and, of course, all the health benefits of honey—these syrups aren't really too bad an indulgence for those of us who occasionally need a more exciting departure from the usual unsweetened seltzer. Or for kids, who might otherwise be begging, pleading, constantly imploring you to give them soda and other sugary drinks, *pleeeaaasssse!!!!!!*

I, for one, went from being the "meanest mommy in the whole wide world" (so many "no"s) to "the goodest mommy ever" just by stirring some of this into my kids' "bubble water." So, who knows the ranks to which you might ascend if you crank out a batch or two of this stuff?! To make homemade soda, first you'll need to make a batch of this incredibly easy honey simple syrup.

SIMPLE SYRUP

1 cup water
1 cup honey

1. Heat the water in a small saucepan or microwave-safe container until steaming but not boiling.

2. Pour in the honey and stir until fully dissolved.

Next comes the fun part: dreaming up soda flavors! The following are a few simple formulas in broad flavor categories. Use both your imagination and the ingredients available to you to make these syrups your own.

Honey-Herb Syrup

Combine one batch of still-warm honey syrup with three sprigs of any fresh herb, steep for 20 to 30 minutes, then strain and cool.

Suggestions: lemon verbena, rosemary, fresh mint, lemon basil, lavender

Honey-Fruit Syrup

Combine one batch of still-warm honey syrup with 8 ounces of peeled and chopped or mashed fruit and 1 teaspoon vanilla extract (optional), steep for 20 to 30 minutes, then strain and cool.

Suggestions: Strawberry, sour cherry, peach, mango, pineapple

Honey-Citrus Syrup

Combine one batch of still-warm honey syrup with ½ cup of fresh citrus juice and 1 tablespoon citrus zest, steep for 20 to 30 minutes, then strain and cool.

Suggestions: Lemon, lime, Meyer lemon, grapefruit, blood orange

Continued

Honey-Spice Syrup

Combine one batch of still-warm honey syrup with ¼ cup of whole dried spices or ½ cup of a chopped fresh spice (e.g., ginger), steep for 20 to 30 minutes, then strain and cool. **Suggestions:** Ginger, allspice, cinnamon, peppercorn, cloves

HOMEMADE SODA

When pouring yourself a cold one, don't feel compelled to stick to one flavor note. Mixing and matching is half the fun when making homemade soda. You can do this by either blending a couple of different syrup flavors when mixing up a glass of soda, or creating flavor blends when making the syrups themselves by steeping the ingredients together. Either way: here are a few flavor combinations that I like, but play around and have fun exploring what you like to drink!

Cherry-Vanilla
Pineapple-Mint
Peach-Ginger
Lemon-Lime
Raspberry-Apricot
Blood Orange–Rosemary
Strawberry-Basil

Whatever flavor train you decide to jump on, here's the recipe for one glass of soda.

1 to 3 tablespoons flavored syrup
Seltzer

1. Fill a tall glass with ice.

2. Add the flavored syrup, then top with seltzer.

3. Stir gently and enjoy!

Note: If you like your sodas a little on the tart side, consider adding a tablespoon of fresh lemon or lime juice to the glass along with the syrup, before topping with seltzer. My husband—a fan of aromatic cocktail bitters—also likes to add a dash or two to his honey sodas, so you could give that a whirl, too.

HONEY LEMON ICED TEA

I didn't really grow up drinking iced tea in the summertime. We were more of an occasional lemonade–sipping kind of family. But I have spent some time in the South, where sweet tea is so popular that it seems to run from the faucet. And I kind of understand why. The tannic tea balanced with sweet sugar is quenching, plus the idea of a big pitcher perpetually chilling in the fridge, ready for whoever happens to come by, is thoroughly hospitable. Besides, a little something sweet and a little something cold alongside a plate of spicy barbecue makes perfect sense to me. So I've been sold. But—purists, please forgive me—I like to swap out the sugar for honey not only because it adds a bit of nutritional oomph to the drink, but it offers depth and flavor interest. The lemon keeps it from being cloying and adds a brightness, too, that creates a more balanced beverage. So, when the weather heats up where you are, you'll see that there's nothing quite like a glass of this newfangled sweet iced tea to cool you down.

Serves 8

8 cups water

6 tea bags black tea

½ cup honey

1 lemon, sliced into ¼-inch rounds, plus more for garnish if desired

Mint for garnish (optional)

1. Place 4 cups of water in a medium saucepan and bring to a simmer. Remove from the heat, add the tea bags, and steep

for 5 to 10 minutes, depending on how strong you like your tea. Remove the tea bags and add the honey. Stir until thoroughly blended. Let cool.

2. Place the sweetened tea, lemon slices, 4 remaining cups of water, and 2 cups of ice in a pitcher. Stir gently.

3. Pour into glasses over ice and garnish with a lemon slice and mint, if desired.

MANGO AND HONEY LASSI

What's *lassi*? you may wonder. It's a traditional sweet and tangy, sometimes spiced and/or salty yogurt-based drink from India. Mango is one of my favorite lassi flavors, but this recipe is delicious with most fruits or, honestly, no fruit at all. A splash of rose water and/or a pinch of ground cardamom are lovely but thoroughly optional, as the sweet honey and mango are just perfect on their own against the tart and creamy yogurt. A lassi is a great way to start the day, but it's also a delightful accompaniment to a spicy meal or enjoyed as a light and refreshing drinkable dessert.

Serves 2

1½ cups plain yogurt
½ cup ice-cold water
1 cup peeled and cubed fresh or frozen mango
2 tablespoons honey
Pinch of salt
¼ teaspoon rose water (optional)
A few ice cubes, for serving (optional)
Pinch of ground cardamom (optional)
Mint for garnish (optional)

1. Place the yogurt, water, mango, honey, salt, and rose water (if using) in a blender. Blend until smooth and creamy. Taste and adjust the sweetness, if desired.

2. Serve in tall glasses over ice (if using). Garnish with a sprinkle of cardamom and mint, if desired.

MAINS

HONEY LEMON ROAST CHICKEN (IN THE SLOW COOKER. OR NOT.)

A good roast chicken is one of life's great delights. Deeply browned, with salty, crackly skin; moist, juicy, tender meat; and an incomparable smell that is the aromatic equivalent of a warm hug, it is, without a doubt, my most favorite way to make chicken. And sometimes all it takes is some heavy-handed salt and peppering to get the job done. But when I have the urge for a bird with a little more depth and flavor, I opt for marinating the chicken in lemon juice for a few hours before roasting it and then burnishing it with honey toward the end of its cooking time. The acid in the lemon not only adds a subtle counterbalance to the honey's deep sweetness, but it also actually tenderizes the meat.

This recipe is 90 percent hands-off, save for the mixing of the marinade and brushing-on of the honey. Then, it's just a matter of letting your oven do the work. Still, there are times when you just can't hang around to babysit a roast chicken, and that's when the set-it-and-forget-it beauty of the slow cooker comes in, allowing you to go about your day and come home to a comforting roast chicken. Truth be told, the skin will not crisp much in the slow cooker, but for crackly skin devotees, there's a reasonably acceptable hack that will satisfy: simply transfer the slow-cooked chicken to a baking dish and pop it under your oven's broiler for three to five minutes before serving.

Serves 4–6

Continued

One 4-pound chicken

Kosher salt

1 cup fresh lemon juice

Freshly ground black pepper

A few sprigs of fresh herbs, such as thyme or rosemary

2 tablespoons olive oil

¼ cup honey

½ lemon, cut into wedges

1. Rub the entire surface of the chicken with about 2 teaspoons of kosher salt. Place the salted chicken and lemon juice in a resealable plastic bag, seal the bag, and shake it gently to distribute the lemon juice. Refrigerate for 2 to 8 hours to marinate.

2. Remove the chicken from the marinade and gently pat dry. Season the cavity generously with salt and pepper, then stuff with fresh herbs. Rub the skin with olive oil, then season generously all over with salt and pepper. Truss the chicken or tie the legs with twine.

To roast in a slow cooker:

1. Roll aluminum foil into three balls, each about 2 inches in diameter, and place them in the bottom of your slow cooker. Place the chicken, breast side up, on top of the foil balls so that it's not sitting directly on the bottom of the slow cooker.

2. Cover the slow cooker, set it to HIGH, and cook for 2½ to 3½ hours; or set to LOW and cook for 5 to 7 hours, until the

chicken is cooked through and an instant-read thermometer inserted into the thickest part of the thigh reads 165°F.

3. Heat the honey in the microwave or in a small saucepan until liquefied, then generously brush it onto the top and sides of the chicken. If the slow cooker is set to LOW, turn it to HIGH and continue to cook for another 10 to 15 minutes.

4. To crisp the skin, carefully transfer the chicken to a baking sheet or baking dish and place under the broiler for 3 to 5 minutes, keeping an eye on the honey, which can burn if left for too long.

5. Remove the twine and transfer the chicken to a platter or carving board. Allow to rest for 10 minutes.

6. Serve with lemon wedges.

To roast in the oven:

1. Preheat the oven to 450°F.

2. Place the chicken in a small roasting pan fitted with a rack or in a large cast-iron skillet. Roast for 20 minutes, then lower the oven temperature to 350°F and roast for another 45 minutes.

3. Heat the honey in the microwave or in a small saucepan until liquefied, then generously brush it onto the top and sides of the chicken. Roast for another 10 to 15 minutes, until an instant-read thermometer inserted into the thickest part of the thigh reads 165°F.

Continued

4. Remove the twine and transfer the chicken to a platter or carving board. Allow to rest for 10 minutes.

5. Serve with lemon wedges.

HONEY-HOISIN MEATBALLS

These meatballs are the little black dress of the ground meat world. They just *work*, no matter what. What I mean is this: they make a great weeknight dinner—add rice and some steamed greens—but they're also fabulous party fare, served on toothpicks alongside a cocktail. Plus, they're great finger food for little ones who are just getting going on the self-feeding front. Sweet, savory, complex, and super simple to make, they're ready in less than half an hour. You can make them big; you can make them small. You can double the batch and freeze half, because they reheat like a dream and will undoubtedly save your butt one day when you find yourself faced with a hungry family and—*somehow*—no dinner plan. Oh, and the leftovers? Well, if you have any, they'll definitely find a good home in a sandwich.

Makes about 24 meatballs

MEATBALLS:

1 pound ground beef, pork, turkey, or a combination

1 tablespoon hoisin sauce

2 tablespoons soy sauce

1 tablespoon minced fresh ginger

2 garlic cloves, minced

1 scallion, thinly sliced

1 teaspoon toasted sesame oil

1 tablespoon honey

½ cup panko bread crumbs

1 large egg, lightly beaten

Continued

GLAZE:

¼ cup hoisin sauce

1 tablespoon ketchup

2 tablespoons honey

2 tablespoons rice vinegar

1 teaspoon toasted sesame oil

1 tablespoon soy sauce

1. Adjust the oven rack to the center position and preheat the oven to 375°F.

2. Place all the meatball ingredients in a large mixing bowl and, using your hands, mix together until blended.

3. Form the meat mixture into 1- to 1½-tablespoon-size meatballs.

4. Place the balls about an inch apart on a parchment-lined baking sheet. Bake for 15 to 20 minutes, until cooked through.

5. Meanwhile, combine all the glaze ingredients in a small saucepan. Bring to a simmer over medium heat, stirring frequently, and cook for 5 to 7 minutes, until the mixture is slightly thickened. Set aside.

6. Brush or pour the glaze over the meatballs. Serve.

SHEET-PAN HONEY MUSTARD SALMON

I dig one-dish meals. Dinner in the slow cooker, one-pot pasta suppers, casseroles, and main dish soups—I love 'em all. It may not seem very chef-y of me to say so, but my favorite of the one-stop-dinnertime-shopping methods just might be the sheet-pan dinner, wherein all of a meal's components are dumped onto a sheet pan, roasted to perfection, and served. It's a fast and healthy way to get a meal on the table and—the best part—there's almost no cleanup. One pan, people. One. Pan. Here I suggest pairing sweet and tangy salmon with thinly sliced potatoes and green beans, but feel free to swap them out for accompaniments that suit your taste, such as asparagus and sweet potatoes or zucchini and chickpeas. Just make sure to select ingredients that will cook at roughly the same rate as the salmon.

Serves 4

¼ cup honey

3 tablespoons Dijon mustard

1 tablespoon apple cider vinegar

1 teaspoon kosher salt

Freshly ground black pepper

Four 6-ounce skin-on salmon fillets, preferably about
    1¼ inches thick

1 pound green beans, trimmed

8 red potatoes (really, any potato will work), cut into
    ¼-inch-thick slices

1 tablespoon olive oil

1. Preheat the oven to 425°F. While the oven is heating, place a foil-lined rimmed baking sheet on the center rack of the oven.

2. Place the honey, mustard, vinegar, ½ teaspoon of the salt, and pepper to taste in a small bowl and whisk. Pour into a resealable plastic bag and add the salmon. Seal the bag and shake gently to distribute the marinade. Refrigerate for 10 to 15 minutes.

3. When the oven comes to temperature, carefully remove the hot baking sheet and place the green beans and pota- toes on the foil. Toss the vegetables with the olive oil and remaining ½ teaspoon of salt. Using a spatula or large spoon, gently slide the vegetables to the sides of the pan to make a space for the salmon in the center of the pan. Remove the salmon from the marinade and place, skin side down, on the pan.

4. Roast for 10 to 12 minutes, until the salmon is cooked through and flakes easily.

GARLIC HONEY SHRIMP SKEWERS

It is an indisputable fact that food on a stick is more fun to eat than food not on a stick. It is also an indisputable fact that shrimp gone wrong is more wrong than many other kinds of wrong. Right? Shrimp that's rubbery, tough, dry or mushy—it's just so very bad. But these shrimp? These shrimp are flavorful, plump, tender, sweet, and spicy. And they're on a stick, so they're fun. Fun shrimp! Woo-hoo! The sauce is what I'd call Korean-ish, as I suggest using *gochujang*, a Korean red pepper paste, to get the hot part of the sweet-hot thing happening. If you can't get your hands on gochujang (available at just about any Asian market and well-stocked grocery store), feel free to sub a tablespoon of red pepper flakes mixed with ¼ teaspoon of soy sauce and ¼ teaspoon of honey. You could even just give it a healthy squirt of sriracha. The flavor won't be exactly the same, but it'll still be damn good. One quick tip when grilling shrimp: packing the shrimp tightly together on the skewers helps to keep them from drying out, so don't be afraid to get cozy while kebab-ing.

Serves 4

1½ pounds large shrimp, peeled and deveined (frozen and
thawed is okay)

¼ teaspoon baking soda

1 teaspoon kosher salt

1 tablespoon gochujang (see headnote)

1 tablespoon honey

2 teaspoons rice vinegar

2 teaspoons soy sauce

½ teaspoon toasted sesame oil

1 small clove garlic, minced

½ teaspoon grated fresh ginger

Olive oil for brushing

1 teaspoon sesame seeds

2 tablespoons thinly sliced scallions

Continued

1. Have ready eight long metal or wooden skewers. If using wooden, soak in water for at least 2 hours to prevent their burning on the grill.

2. Combine the shrimp, baking soda, and salt in a medium bowl. Toss to coat. Thread the shrimp onto paired skewers (both skewers should pass through each shrimp, to keep it flat), pushing the shrimp together along the skewers so that no space remains between the shrimp. You should have four sets of shrimp-laden skewers in all. Refrigerate for 30 minutes.

3. Meanwhile, combine the gochujang, honey, vinegar, soy sauce, sesame oil, garlic, and ginger in a small bowl. Mix well.

4. Heat a cleaned and oiled outdoor grill to the highest heat setting (or heat a grill pan on your indoor stove for 10 minutes). Place the shrimp directly onto the grill and cook, turning occasionally, until the shrimp are just beginning to char, about 3 minutes. Brush the glaze onto both sides of the shrimp, and cook for no more than 60 to 90 seconds more, until the shrimp are opaque and just cooked through.

5. Transfer to a platter, brush with any remaining glaze, and top with sesame seeds and scallions. Serve immediately.

WHY BAKING SODA?

Baking soda's alkaline pH helps the shrimp brown more quickly so flavor comes sooner, before the shrimp has a chance to go rubbery-wrong. For more on this and other cool uses for baking soda, see my book *The Baking Soda Companion*.

CHICKEN-FRIED CAULIFLOWER WITH HOT HONEY DRIZZLE

We've been trying to eat a more plant-based diet in our house lately. Health, the environment, yadda yadda—it's a good idea. And it seems to suit us, as we are—in general—a household of willing fruit and vegetable eaters. We haven't eschewed animal products altogether, but we've definitely cut way back. On animal products. Not on flavor. Take this cauliflower dish, for example. I spent some formative childhood years living in the South and have a love for fried chicken that runs deep, so I know when it's good. I also know that to fry something other than chicken—say, cauliflower—and then claim it's "as good as fried chicken" is completely ridiculous. I'm not making that claim. (I'm not ridiculous!) *But* this cauliflower—fried a bit as one would fry chicken—*is* delicious: crunchy, salty, surprisingly meaty, and, thanks to the hot honey drizzle, sticky, tangy, spicy, and—dare I say it—finger lickin' good.

Serves 4

1 cup buttermilk

1 tablespoon salt

¼ cup hot sauce (optional)

1 head cauliflower, cut into 1½-inch florets

3 large eggs, lightly beaten

1½ cups all-purpose flour

2 teaspoons freshly ground black pepper, or more to taste

¼ teaspoon cayenne pepper

Continued

½ teaspoon garlic powder

½ teaspoon onion powder

½ teaspoon smoked paprika

1 teaspoon dried oregano

1 tablespoon baking powder

Vegetable or corn oil for frying

HOT HONEY DRIZZLE:

¼ cup honey

¼ teaspoon cayenne pepper, or more to taste

1. Combine the buttermilk, 1 teaspoon of the salt, and the hot sauce (if using) in a large, airtight container. Add the cauliflower florets; turn to coat. Cover and refrigerate for 2 hours or overnight.

2. When ready to fry, set up a dredging station: Put the beaten eggs and flour into separate shallow bowls or plates. Mix the remaining 2 teaspoons of salt and the pepper, cayenne, garlic powder, onion powder, paprika, oregano, and baking powder with the flour. Dip the cauliflower florets, a few at a time, into the flour mixture until coated completely. Toss the flour-coated cauliflower pieces into the eggs until they're well coated, then return them to the flour mixture and toss again. Shake off any excess, then transfer the coated pieces to a platter or baking sheet. Let stand for 30 minutes.

3. Meanwhile, preheat a tabletop fryer or a large Dutch oven filled with 2 to 3 inches of oil to 350°F on a deep-frying

thermometer. (Or follow your air fryer's instruction manual.)

4. Working in batches of four or five pieces (don't overcrowd the pan), fry the cauliflower for 2 to 3 minutes, until the outside is golden brown and the inside is tender.

5. Use a slotted spoon or tongs to transfer the cooked florets to a paper towel–lined tray to drain. Once all the pieces are cooked, transfer to a serving platter.

6. Prepare the honey drizzle: Place the honey in a small saucepan and warm over low heat. Stir in the cayenne, adding more if desired. Drizzle the warm honey over the cauliflower. Serve immediately.

Note: This recipe is not 100 percent plant-based, but can be easily converted as follows: instead of 1 cup of buttermilk, use 1 cup of unsweetened plant-based milk combined with 1 teaspoon of apple cider vinegar; instead of the 3 eggs, use 3 tablespoons of ground flaxseeds combined with 6 tablespoons of water.

HONEY GINGER BEEF TACOS WITH PINEAPPLE SALSA

My family is pretty into tacos. I wouldn't go so far as to describe us as "obsessed," but I think it's safe to say that we're taco superfans. I make tacos for dinner *at least* once a week and the mere sight of the toppings spread on the table never fails to elicit actual squeals of delight from my kids upon realizing that tacos are coming. Somewhat recently, however, I realized I was in a bit of a taco rut, rarely veering away from my children's—*ahem*—"selective" preference for the ground turkey/shredded chicken filling I was making all the time. My people would *occasionally* go for ground beef or maaaaybe an egg taco here or there, but the chicken/turkey pothole was real and I was B-O-R-E-D. These complex, faintly Asian-y, thoroughly delicious tacos saved me from myself and brought back the excitement to taco night. I'm a big fan of a long, slow braise on a Sunday afternoon, especially when the days are shorter and the weather is crisp. The smell! Mmmmmm. And this recipe certainly scratches that itch. But, in case you're wondering, yes—this dish is definitely slow cooker–friendly, so it's also thoroughly doable on a weeknight (Taco Tuesday isn't just for the school cafeteria menu, you know) and is a welcome no-oven summertime supper. See the recipe notes for a how-to.

Serves 4 to 6

Continued

BEEF:

One 2- to 3-pound boneless beef chuck roast, or 2 to 3 pounds
   boneless short ribs

Kosher salt

Freshly ground black pepper

2 tablespoons olive oil

1 small onion, thinly sliced

5 garlic cloves, minced

1 tablespoon grated fresh ginger

1 cup beef or chicken stock

⅓ cup soy sauce

¾ cup honey

Corn or flour tortillas

SALSA:

2 cups fresh pineapple, peeled, cored, and diced small

1 teaspoon finely minced jalapeño pepper

¼ cup diced red bell pepper

¼ cup minced red onion

½ cup cilantro, roughly chopped

Zest and juice of 1 small lime

⅛ teaspoon kosher salt

1. Preheat the oven to 325°F.

2. Season the beef *generously* on all sides with kosher salt and
   black pepper.

3. Heat the olive oil in a large Dutch oven over medium-high
   heat until shimmering. Cook the beef until well browned
   on all sides, 8 to 10 minutes total. Transfer to a plate.

4. Add the onion to the Dutch oven and cook until it begins to soften, about 5 minutes. Add the garlic and ginger and cook for another minute.

5. Return the roast to the Dutch oven. Add the stock, soy sauce, and honey and bring to a simmer.

6. Place the lid on the pot and transfer to the oven. Cook, turning occasionally, for 3½ hours, or until fork-tender.

7. To prepare the salsa, place all the salsa ingredients in a small bowl. Toss well to combine.

8. Remove the beef from the oven and allow it to rest for 10 minutes, then shred with two forks. Serve with warm tortillas (heated in a dry skillet for 30 seconds) and pineapple salsa.

To prepare in a slow cooker: Lightly grease the bottom and sides of a slow cooker. Add the beef (seasoned generously with salt and pepper), then add the onion, garlic, ginger, soy sauce, honey and only ½ cup of stock to the slow cooker and cook on high for 3 to 4 hours, or until fall-apart tender.

HONEY LIME SKILLET CHICKEN THIGHS

I've never really understood the popularity of chicken breasts. Sure, people say they're "healthier" than dark meat (because they're lower in fat, but the difference is so negligible, people!) and some would argue in favor of their versatility, but I have to go with thighs when choosing my chicken (and I think you should, too). Here's why: they're juicer, much more flavorful, and, frankly, much harder to mess up. Plus, they're typically less expensive—a bonus. This recipe gives my favorite and too-often-overlooked piece of chicken the love it deserves. Start it, skin side down, in a cold skillet so it gets nice and crispy. Then, hoist up the heat and roast it in the oven until it's perfectly cooked. Using a single skillet and everyday ingredients, this is definitely a fine answer to weeknight busyness.

Serves 4

2 pounds bone-in, skin-on chicken thighs (4 to 6 thighs)

¼ cup fresh lime juice

2 tablespoons honey

1 tablespoon soy sauce

2 tablespoons olive oil

½ teaspoon salt

Freshly ground black pepper

2 scallions, white and green parts, thinly sliced

1. Arrange a rack in the middle of the oven and preheat the oven to 400°F.

2. Combine the lime juice, honey, and soy sauce in a small bowl. Mix well.

3. Drizzle the chicken thighs with the olive oil and season well with the salt and pepper.

4. Place the thighs, skin side down, in a single layer in a large, *cold* cast-iron skillet. Place the skillet over medium heat and cook for 14 to 15 minutes, until the skin is crispy and browned. Turn the chicken and pour the honey mixture over the thighs.

5. Transfer the skillet to the oven and roast until the chicken reaches an internal temperature of 165°F, about 15 minutes. Serve immediately, garnished with the scallions.

NEXT-LEVEL GRILLED CHEESE WITH HONEY

Host: Welcome to Food Jeopardy, *America's most popular answer-and-question show! Yes, we give the answers, and then it's up to you to come up with the questions. Contestants, put your hands on the buzzers, but please don't ring in until the answer is revealed. Our first category is Comfort Foods and—ready—here's your first answer: Rainy days, a head cold, a hangover, and a broken heart.*

(ding-ding)

Contestant 1: What are "predicaments that can only be cured by a grilled cheese sandwich?"

Host: You are absolutely correct. Congratulations!

Yes, it's a game show–worthy fact that grilled cheese is pretty much the cure for whatever ails you. And while one could very reasonably argue that classic grilled cheese is a nearly perfect food, requiring little to no improvement, it is actually possible to take this humble fare up a notch with just a few teensy twists. In this recipe, Gruyère and honey combine to bring sweet and savory together in perfect harmony. It's so simple, but also crazy good. Take this classic even further by stuffing it with caramelized onions or apple slices, or by switching up the cheese for fresh mozzarella, Taleggio, Manchego, or whatever you like.

Serves 4

4 tablespoons (½ stick) unsalted butter, at room temperature

8 slices sourdough bread or another bread of your choosing

1 pound Gruyère, sliced

About 4 teaspoons honey for drizzling

Coarse sea salt

Coarsely ground black pepper

1. Heat a griddle or two large skillets over medium heat until hot.

2. For each sandwich, place one-quarter of the cheese on top of one bread slice, drizzle with 1 teaspoon of the honey, and top with a second bread slice. Spread the outsides of each sandwich with 1 tablespoon of the butter.

3. Place on the griddle, lower the heat to medium-low, and cook until the undersides are golden brown, 3 to 4 minutes. Flip the sandwiches and brown the other side, 3 to 4 minutes more. Serve at once, drizzling with more honey if you like, and seasoning with coarse sea salt and fresh black pepper to taste.

DRESSINGS, DRIZZLES, SPREADS, AND SAUCES

ALL-PURPOSE SWEET AND TANGY SALAD DRESSING

This recipe is the perfect way to put an *almost* empty jar of honey to good use. It is so simple to make it's hardly a recipe at all—just dump all of the ingredients into a nearly empty honey jar, shake well, and . . . voilà! The dressing can be stored in the fridge for a couple of weeks, but it's probably going to be gone long before then.

Makes about 1 cup

¾ cup olive oil

¼ cup fresh lemon juice

2 teaspoons Dijon mustard

1 to 2 teaspoons honey—or whatever is left in the jar

Kosher salt and freshly ground black pepper

Place all the ingredients into your honey jar (or another empty jar) and shake.

JAMMY HONEY-ROASTED TOMATOES

I'm a big fan of the BLT. Really, any kind of tomato sandwich does it for me. Toasted bread with some olive oil/mayo/bacon/what-have-you; a thick, juicy slab of perfect in-season tomato; a sprinkling of salt and pepper; and, sure, throw some lettuce on there, too, please—that's perfection. Alas, the heart wants what the heart wants and in moments of desperation, against my better judgment, I have made the mistake of ordering a BLT at a restaurant in the dead of winter (Why?!) and I learned my lesson. Adding a mealy, pale slice of tomato—the ingredient that *should* actually be the star of the sandwich—is a quick and surefire way to ruin lunch. While I understand and fully support the notion that a BLT or tomato sandwich should be a seasonal treat, I am not opposed to finding loopholes in the name of off-season gratification. This sorta tomato jam is just the kind of loophole I'm talking about. Its sweet, summery, dreamy tomato flavor added to a sandwich (or a cheeseboard, or a plate of eggs . . .) can fulfill that hankering pretty well. And the best news is that it works beautifully with those not-great fresh tomatoes that are lurking around when the air is cold, so it's truly a year-round recipe hack!

Makes about 1 cup

1 pint cherry, grape, or other small variety of tomatoes, halved

2 tablespoons minced onion

1 tablespoon honey

3 tablespoons olive oil, plus more for pan

¼ teaspoon salt

Freshly ground black pepper

1. Preheat the oven to 375°F. Grease or line a baking sheet with parchment paper or foil.

2. Combine the tomatoes, onion, honey, olive oil, salt, and pepper to taste in a bowl. Toss well to evenly coat the tomatoes.

3. Spread the tomatoes on the prepared pan, making sure not to space them too far apart—they like to remain cozy. You want a little huddle of tomatoes in the center of the pan.

4. Roast for 20 to 30 minutes, until lightly browned and bubbling.

CHILE-INFUSED HONEY (PLUS OTHER INFUSIONS YOU'LL LOVE)

A few years ago, someone gifted us a bottle of chile pepper–infused honey that we seriously couldn't stop eating. We tried it on pizza, popcorn, salmon, soft pretzels, sandwiches, plain yogurt, in cocktails, and right off the spoon . . . until the bottle ran out. At that point, I began to wonder, *How hard can it possibly be to make my own hot honey?* And thus began my honey-infusing mania. As I learned, infusing honey with herbs, spices, and even fruits is dead-easy and is a great way to give all manner of dishes a little more depth, a little more flavor, a little more sumpin'. Plus, a jar of infused honey makes a great gift (see above), so keep a few extras in your cabinet and bring one along next time you're invited out for dinner.

Makes about 1 cup

5 dried New Mexican red chiles (or other dried chiles of your choosing), or 2 tablespoons red pepper flakes
1 cup honey

1. Place the dried chiles in the bottom of a glass jar.

2. Warm the honey in a saucepan over very low heat, until liquefied and hot.

3. Pour the warmed honey into the jar over the chiles. Allow to cool completely before covering the jar with its lid.

4. Allow the honey to sit for 5 to 7 days or longer (longer = stronger flavor) at room temperature before using.

5. Once infused, you can strain it into a clean glass jar. Store at room temperature indefinitely.

Suggestions: To make other infused honeys, swap out the dried chiles for 2 tablespoons of dried herbs, spices, or chopped dried fruit. I happen to like using cinnamon sticks, whole cardamom, star anise, chamomile, vanilla bean, and rosemary—sometimes on their own and sometimes in different combinations with one another. Have fun experimenting with flavors you love, then try your infused honey stirred into tea, added to salad dressing, served along with cheese, and—yes—drizzled on pizza. But please note: use only dried flavorings (as opposed to fresh herbs, for example), when making infused honey, to mitigate any risk of bacterial growth.

WHIPPED HONEY BUTTER

I love butter—for better or worse—and use it often enough to have educated my family on the notion that it is a Very Important Food. Even my four-year-old regularly repeats the mantra "Everything's better with butter." When my husband and I were dating seriously, after we'd learned all about each other's families and childhoods and hopes and dreams for the future, I remember becoming (maniacally?) focused on trying to figure out his food quirks, because this stuff is important when you're considering spending a lifetime with another person. At some point, I started to notice that he didn't really like butter or mayonnaise or whipped cream or, really, anything creamy (ice cream excepted). *Okay*, I thought, I didn't necessarily *understand* the whipped cream thing, but I could work with it. And mayonnaise is definitely one of those inexplicably polarizing foods, so I accepted that one, too. But the butter thing stopped me in my tracks and I actually found myself wondering, *Can I spend the rest of my life with someone who doesn't like butter?* Thankfully, I didn't have to find out, because slowly, over time, I've ~~worn him down~~ shown him the light. There are still some things that are "too buttery" for him, such as puff pastry (whuh?!), but he has come to appreciate and accept butter in enough other places that it doesn't matter. This whipped honey, for example, is something he loves. And who wouldn't? It's creamy, sweet, and salty. The Big Three. It's perfect on anything from toast to just-out-of-the-oven corn bread to pancakes and waffles. I defy you to find a butter-skeptic who doesn't love this stuff.

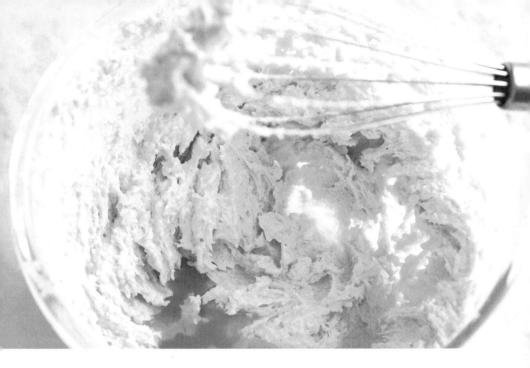

Makes about 1 cup

½ pound (2 sticks) salted butter, softened
3 tablespoons honey
Sea salt, if desired

1. Place the butter in a large bowl or the bowl of a stand mixer. Using a handheld mixer or the stand mixer fitted with a paddle attachment, beat the butter for 1 minute on medium speed, or until smooth and creamy. Scrape down the sides of the bowl with a rubber spatula.

2. Add the honey and beat again until combined. Taste and add a little sea salt if the mixture isn't quite salty enough for you. Serve.

3. Honey butter can be stored, covered, in the refrigerator for up to 2 weeks. Bring to room temperature before serving.

CREAMED HONEY

Smooth, "buttery," drip-less, spreadable and—uh—*creamy*, creamed honey is a treat on toast, bagels, biscuits, and more. For years, I assumed it was simply runny honey that had been whisked into something stiff yet light, sort of like what happens to egg whites when they're whipped, but it's actually more akin to making sourdough bread or yogurt: with a starter. Creamed honey, as it turns out, is simply crystallized, but in a way that is controlled and results in tiny, round little crystals rather than the big, gritty ones that occur naturally when honey hangs around for a while.

Transforming liquid honey to creamed is easy: all you do is beat a little creamed honey (either from a store-bought batch or an older homemade stash) into "regular" honey, wait a week, and presto!—creamed honey, ready for toast, peanut butter sandwiches, or—my favorite—licking off a spoon!

Make about 1 cup

1 cup liquid honey

2 tablespoons seed honey (already creamed honey)

1. Place both honeys in the bowl of a stand mixer fitted with the paddle attachment or using a handheld electric mixer and beat until thoroughly combined.

2. Pour the mixture into a glass jar and cover with its lid. Store it in a cool, dark place (but not the fridge!!) until the mixture has fully "creamed," about a week and a half.

You'll know when it's happened because the color of the honey will be much lighter and the contents of the jar will stay put when tilted.

3. Creamed honey will last indefinitely and, amazingly, will never get grainy.

BAKED AND
SWEET THINGS

3-INGREDIENT CARAMEL SAUCE

A jar of homemade caramel sauce is one of those things that will talk to you from the other side of the fridge door. You know, like, "Pssst! Yoo-hoo! I'm in hee-eere. Remember how delicious I am? Dontcha want another spoonful of me? Come onnnnn." Oh, is that just my fridge? Can't be. Either way, thick, rich, and impossibly smooth, this is really good stuff, more complex than your average caramel; and can I say it's healthier because of the honey—or is that taking things too far? Maybe just a tad. It's delicious spooned into yogurt with a little fruit, used as a dip for apple slices, drizzled over ice cream (duh), or stirred into coffee (really!). The sauce should be served warm and can be stored in a jar in the refrigerator for up to 2 weeks. (Hahahaha—like it's going to hang around for that long!)

Makes about 1½ cups

1 cup heavy whipping cream
½ cup honey
4 tablespoons (½ stick) salted butter
Generous pinch of flaked sea salt

1. Place the cream, honey, butter, and salt in a medium to large saucepan (use a much larger pot than you think you need). Bring to a boil over medium heat, whisking until mixture is thoroughly combined.

2. Let the mixture continue to boil for 5 to 8 minutes, stirring or swirling the pot now and then to prevent burning,

Continued

until it turns a deep amber color. As soon as it reaches the desired color, immediately remove the pan from the heat.

3. Let the caramel cool for about 20 minutes, then serve.

4. The sauce can be stored in an airtight container in the refrigerator for up to 2 weeks. Reheat in a small pot over low heat, or place in a microwave-safe container and microwave on full power at 30-second intervals.

PEANUT BUTTER AND HONEY GRANOLA

Say hello to the easiest granola you'll ever make. Trust me. I've made *a lot* of granola at home over the years, on a quest to come up with a recipe I loved—one that wasn't too sweet, too fussy (3 different cooking methods and 16 ingredients? No thank you!), or . . . well, annoying. Plus it had to be delicious. At the end of the day, what I wanted was to be able to dump a few ingredients into a bowl, mix it up, and end up with the crunchy, chewy, sweet, and a little bit salty granola of my dreams. Well, believe it or not, this simple, straightforward, super-customizable recipe is pretty much that!

You can definitely use any kind of nut butter you like—I just happen to like the combination of peanut butter and honey, because it reminds me of one of my favorite lunchbox sandwiches. Want a PB&J-inspired granola instead? Toss some raisins and dried strawberries into the finished product. Think the only thing missing from this recipe is a little chocolate? You might not be wrong about that and can find out for yourself by adding anywhere from ½ to ¾ cup of chocolate chips to a thoroughly cooled batch. What I'm trying to say is this is a really good base to play around with. Switch up the nuts, swap out the dried fruit (or skip it entirely), toss in a teaspoon or so of your favorite spices. You can't mess this up.

Makes about 8 cups

Continued

4 cups old-fashioned rolled oats

2 cups peanuts or any combination of other nuts and/or seeds

1 teaspoon kosher salt

½ teaspoon ground cinnamon

½ cup olive oil

½ cup honey

¾ cup natural peanut butter

¾ cup raisins or other dried fruit

1. Preheat the oven to 350°F. Line a large baking sheet with parchment paper.

2. Combine the oats, peanuts, salt, cinnamon, olive oil, honey, and peanut butter in a large bowl. Stir thoroughly. You're going to need to put a little bit of muscle into it!

3. Spread the oat mixture evenly on the prepared baking sheet and bake for 20 to 25 minutes, stirring halfway through the baking time to ensure even browning.

4. Allow the granola to cool, then add the raisins and toss to combine.

Note: If you store your peanut butter in the fridge, you're definitely going to want to soften it up before attempting to stir it into your granola, unless you've got muscles like Ahnold. The easiest way is in the microwave; 30 to 40 seconds on high should do it.

STRUFFOLI

The first time I ever ate *struffoli* was with a bunch of three-year-olds. My daughter was in preschool and had just finished learning about honeybees. Her teacher—a legend in our house and one of my daughter's favorite people of all time—orchestrated a spring-themed celebration, complete with tiny kids clad in cardboard bee costumes, "pollinating" giant construction paper flowers and dancing the "honeybee shuffle." You can't even imagine the cuteness. Off the charts.

After the "show," refreshments were served, including these adorable little, honey-drenched, deep-fried dough balls, which are actually a traditional Italian holiday dessert, struffoli. How did I not know about struffoli?! Sweet, light, citrusy, and festive, it's a food that's all about tradition, celebration, and fun—which, yes, makes perfect sense for holiday celebrations, but is also a genius way to party down with little ones any time. Of course, deep-frying is an adults-only undertaking, but the rest of this recipe is perfectly suited to making with children, who love rolling the dough into teensy marble-size balls and going to town with the decorations. The recipe is easily doubled, making it great for gift-giving.

Serves 6

2 cups all-purpose flour, plus more for dusting

½ teaspoon baking powder

½ teaspoon salt

1 teaspoon finely grated lemon zest

1 teaspoon finely grated orange zest

¼ teaspoon ground cinnamon

3 large eggs, lightly beaten

½ teaspoon vanilla extract

1 cup honey

Vegetable oil for frying

Sprinkles, nonpareils, or colored sugar for garnish

Other traditional garnishes: toasted hazelnuts, maraschino
cherries, candied fruit (optional)

1. Pulse together the flour, baking powder, salt, lemon and
   orange zest, and cinnamon in the bowl of a food processor.
   With the motor running, add the eggs and vanilla and process for about 30 seconds, or until a smooth dough forms.
   Knead the dough on a lightly floured surface for a minute
   or so, then wrap in plastic wrap and let rest at room temperature for 30 minutes.

2. Divide the dough into four equal parts. On a lightly floured
   surface, roll out each piece of dough into ¼-inch-thick rectangle. Cut each rectangle into ½-inch-wide strips. Cut each
   strip into ½-inch pieces and roll each piece into a small
   ball, roughly the size of a hazelnut. Transfer the dough
   pieces to a large, rimmed baking sheet.

3. In the meantime, line another large, rimmed baking sheet
   with a few layers of paper towels. Pour enough oil into a
   large, wide saucepan to come halfway up the sides and
   heat over high heat to 350° to 365°F, until a piece of dough
   sizzles on contact.

Continued

4. Working in batches, and without crowding, add the dough pieces to the hot oil and fry, turning as needed, until they're puffed and golden brown, about 3 minutes. Using a wire skimmer or slotted spoon, transfer the cooked dough balls to the paper towel–lined baking sheet.

5. Heat the honey in a very large saucepan or wide skillet over medium heat until fluid. Add the balls and stir until completely coated. (This will remind you of making crispy rice treats.) Spoon the honey-coated balls onto a serving dish, then decorate with sprinkles and other garnishes (if using). Let cool.

NEW-SCHOOL JEWISH-ISH HONEY CAKE

Honey cake is something traditionally eaten on the Jewish New Year, Rosh Hashanah, because eating sweet things—especially honey—are supposed to encourage a sweet New Year. But for something so customary and, supposedly, so propitious, honey cake sure has gotten a bum rap. It's more or less the Jewish equivalent of the Christmas fruitcake, a "delicacy" on every dessert table that no one will touch. And I tend to agree. Most honey cake I've encountered is dreadfully dry and much too sweet. On a mission to Take Back Honey Cake and design a recipe that worked, I began to think about what needed fixing. *What would balance the excessive sweetness? What would improve the texture? Hang on . . . what's the one thing I can always count on to save dessert when all else fails? CHOCOLATE!* Yep, I completely bastardized the thing, putting chocolate where it doesn't belong. Except it *so* does. I promise you this cake is still deliciously sweet, it's dense (in a good way), moist, and chocolaty in a way that harmonizes with but doesn't overpower the honey. I'm not sure if it's the chocolate cake for honey cake lovers or the honey cake for chocolate lovers, but it's a good cake either way and you should hurry up and make it already, because it's easy and delicious and, for goodness sake, do you really need any other reason to bake something?! Sheesh!

Serves 8 to 10

Continued

CAKE:

Nonstick spray or butter for pan

½ pound (2 sticks) butter, at room temperature

1⅓ cups light brown sugar

2 large eggs

½ cup honey

4 ounces semisweet chocolate, melted and cooled slightly

1 tablespoon unsweetened cocoa powder, sifted

1½ cups all-purpose flour

1 teaspoon baking soda

¼ teaspoon salt

1 cup boiling water

HONEY GANACHE:

8 ounces semisweet chocolate, chips or chopped

1 cup heavy whipping cream

2 tablespoons honey

2 tablespoons cold unsalted butter, cut into pieces

1 tablespoon dark rum or whiskey (optional)

½ teaspoon vanilla extract

1. Position a rack in the center of the oven and preheat the oven to 350°F. Spray or butter a 9-inch-diameter spring-form pan, then line the bottom with parchment paper or greased aluminum foil.

2. Prepare the cake: In a stand mixer fitted with the paddle attachment or in a large bowl, using a handheld electric mixer, beat the butter on medium speed for about a minute. Add the sugar. Increase the mixer speed to high and

beat until light and fluffy, about 2 minutes more. Add the eggs, one at a time, beating well on medium-high speed after each addition. Add the honey and then the melted chocolate, beating just until combined. With the mixer on low speed, gradually add the cocoa powder, flour, baking soda, and salt, scraping down the sides of the bowl as necessary. Slowly and carefully add the boiling water, mixing until just combined.

3. Pour the batter into the prepared pan.

4. Bake, rotating the pan halfway through, until a wooden skewer inserted in the center of the cake comes out with only a few moist crumbs clinging to it, about 60 minutes.

5. Remove from the oven and allow the cake to cool in the pan on a rack for 10 to 15 minutes. Run a knife along the edge of the pan, unclip it, and move the cake onto the rack; let cool completely.

6. Prepare the ganache: Put the chocolate in a heatproof bowl. Combine the cream and honey in a small saucepan over medium-high heat, stirring until the honey dissolves into the cream, about 30 seconds. When the mixture comes to a simmer, remove it from the heat and pour it over the chocolate. Let stand about 1 minute, then whisk until smooth. Whisk in the butter, rum (if using), and vanilla until the butter is melted and the mixture is glossy. Let it set for 10 to 15 minutes.

Continued

If you're impatient, you can glaze the cake like this:

Place the cooled cake on a wire rack set over a baking sheet. Pour the cooled ganache evenly over the top of the cake until it's thoroughly coated. Allow it to set for about 15 minutes.

If you're patient (and congrats on that, by the way), you can frost the cake like this:

Allow the ganache to come to room temperature for at least 8 hours. It will thicken as it cools. (The ganache can actually sit, covered, at room temperature for up to 24 hours.) Once at room temperature, place the ganache in the bowl of a stand mixer and whip on high speed for 2 to 3 minutes. Then, use as you would any other cake frosting, spreading it evenly on the sides and top of the cake.

SHORTCUT BAKLAVA

Baklava, for the uninitiated, is a Middle Eastern and Mediterranean dessert made with layers of buttered phyllo dough and ground nuts, *drenched* in sweet syrup. It's one of those desserts that is somehow both light and rich—it's warm, buttery, nutty, honey-soaked heaven. I have made baklava at home, and while it isn't exactly difficult to do—especially if you're using premade phyllo—it can be really, really time-consuming. My philosophy is that a lack of patience, swiftness, or precision should not come between anyone and a good dessert—as such, a baklava-esque dessert bar that tastes quite a bit like the real thing, but comes together in about half the time (save for the dough-chilling). Feel free to use any combination of nuts here; pistachios, walnuts, or almonds are traditional, but play around with what you like. Same goes for the spices: cinnamon, cloves, and cardamom are typical, but you know what spices you like. Use those. Or don't use any. Also, giving a sprinkling of rose water or orange flower water to the finished product is both authentic and delicious.

Makes 22 to 24 pieces

DOUGH:

Butter for pan

3 cups all-purpose flour, plus more for dusting

8 ounces unsalted butter, cut into small pieces

1 teaspoon baking soda

1 cup sour cream

2 large egg yolks

Continued

FILLING:

1 ⅓ cups honey

1 teaspoon ground cinnamon

¼ teaspoon ground cardamom or cloves (optional)

2 large egg whites

3 cups ground walnuts, pistachios, or almonds

TOPPING:

1 egg yolk, lightly beaten

Whole or ground nuts for garnish

1. Preheat the oven to 350°F. Butter the bottom and sides of a 9-by-13-inch baking dish.

2. Prepare the dough: Pulse together the flour, butter, and baking soda in a food processor until most of the mixture resembles coarse meal. Add the sour cream and egg yolks and pulse just until the mixture holds together and you have a soft dough.

3. Divide the dough into three equal parts, forming each into a thick disk. Wrap each disk separately in plastic wrap and chill in the refrigerator for 1 hour.

4. Meanwhile, prepare the filling: Using a stand mixer or electric handheld mixer, combine the honey, cinnamon, other spices (if using), and egg whites and beat until well blended, about 3 minutes. Add the nuts and stir to combine.

5. Remove the dough from the refrigerator. On a lightly floured surface, roll out each disk of dough into a rectangle roughly the size of your baking dish. Carefully transfer one sheet of the dough to the prepared pan, gently pressing it against the bottom and the sides of the pan. Repair any tears by pressing lightly into the dough.

6. Spread half of the nut filling evenly over the dough layer. Place a second sheet of dough on top of the filling, spread the remaining filling over this layer, then top with the third layer of dough. Press down lightly to smoosh the pastry together.

7. Add the topping: Using a pastry brush, brush the top layer of dough with the beaten egg yolk. Using a sharp knife, carefully cut the baklava into diamond shapes (first cut 4 parallel lengthwise lines, then cut several diagonal lines), cutting all the way to the bottom of the pan. Sprinkle with the additional ground nuts or press whole nuts into the top of each piece, if desired.

8. Bake on the center rack of the oven until golden on top, 30 to 40 minutes. Remove from the oven and allow the baklava to cool completely in the pan before serving. Store the bars in an airtight container at room temperature for up to a week.

EASY HONEY WHOLE WHEAT SANDWICH BREAD

Homemade bread baking has a reputation for being difficult, extremely complicated, and somehow scary. Well, I am here to tell you that it can be none of those things. Sure, making your own sandwich bread takes a little bit of time, but not a lot of effort. And the results are soooo worth it! Name five smells that are better than baking bread. See? You can't! This recipe is truly easy—great for beginner bread bakers—and requires almost no kneading, especially if you have a stand mixer. (If you don't, no worries, it's still super-doable.) But lest you fret that you need to sit around for hours to bake this stuff, worry not—it only takes a few minutes to make the dough, which you could do one night after work, then keep it in the fridge and bake the next night or even a couple days later. And then—oh, baby—you have honey-kissed, warm, and nutty bread, perfect for not-sad-desk-lunch sandwiches, toasted and smeared with Whipped Honey Butter (page 88), or kicked old school with PB&J. The recipe makes two loaves—one for now (how can you resist?) and one for the freezer.

Makes 2 loaves

1 cup lukewarm water

1½ cups milk (any kind), heated until just slightly warm

½ cup honey

1½ tablespoons instant yeast

1 large egg

¼ cup (½ stick) melted butter, vegetable oil, or olive oil, plus a little more to coat bowl

5 cups bread flour (not all-purpose flour)

3 cups whole wheat flour, plus more as needed

1 tablespoon kosher salt

All-purpose flour for dusting

Oil, butter, or nonstick spray for pan

1. Combine the water, milk, honey, and yeast in in the bowl of a stand mixer, or in a large bowl. Stir to incorporate. Add the egg and butter and whisk until mixed. Add the flours and salt and mix together for 1 minute using either the paddle attachment on a stand mixer set on low speed, or by hand, using a large spoon. The dough will be wet and super-shaggy. Let it rest for 5 minutes.

2. Using your mixer's dough hook or continuing to wield your trusty mixing spoon, mix the dough for another 2 minutes. The dough will less shaggy and less wet, but still sticky. If it's really wet, add more whole wheat flour, a spoonful at a time. Continue to mix with the dough hook or by hand for another 3 to 5 minutes, until the dough is smooth and tacky, but not overly sticky.

3. Scrape out the dough onto a lightly floured surface. Clean out the mixing bowl and grease it lightly with a little oil. Form the dough into a ball and turn it in the bowl to coat it with oil. Cover the bowl with plastic wrap and let the dough rise in a warm spot until nearly doubled in bulk, 1 to 1½ hours, or transfer the dough to the fridge and let it

Continued

slowly rise overnight (or longer). (If refrigerating, remove the dough from the fridge about 3 hours before you plan to bake it.)

4. Preheat the oven to 350°F.

5. Grease two 9-by-5-inch loaf pans with oil, softened butter, or a nonstick spray. Sprinkle a little flour on the counter and turn out the dough on top. Divide the dough into two equal parts and shape each into a loaf. Transfer to the loaf pans. Let the loaves rise a second time, until they dome over the rim of the loaf pans, about 30 minutes to an hour.

6. Bake the loaves in the center of the oven for 35 to 40 minutes. The finished loaves will be deeply golden brown and sound hollow when tapped on the bottom. Remove the loaves from the pans and let them cool completely on a baking rack before slicing and/or freezing.

To freeze: Allow the bread to cool completely, then slice the loaf. Wrap tightly in plastic wrap or place in a resealable plastic freezer bag. It will keep in the freezer for 3 to 6 months. To thaw, remove from the freezer and let sit on the countertop until the loaf reaches room temperature. That's it!

PART THREE

HONEY FOR HEALTH

STRESS-RELIEVING TEA

We could all use a little less stress in our lives. Between work, family, and frenzied schedules . . . there's a lot to work through on a day-to-day basis. I don't know about you, but I'm always in search of ways to relax more and stress less. I try to sleep enough; spend time with people I love; exercise; keep my intake of sugar, alcohol, and caffeine to "responsible adult" levels; and generally stay on top of my overall physical and mental health. That said, there's no amount of sleep or group hugs that will make meeting deadlines or troubling global events go away, and sometimes the body's natural alarm switch—the one that controls the "fight or flight" response—gets stuck in the On position. When that happens, it's hard to sleep, it's hard to con-centrate, and—I loathe to admit—it's easy to lose patience with everything and everyone. I wish I could tell you that honey can fix it all. Sorry, folks. Pouring honey on your bills won't make them disappear, but drinking honey tea *can* promote relaxation and help ease you to sleep at night!! Since honey raises our insu-lin slightly and allows tryptophan (the stuff famous for making us sleepy after eating Thanksgiving turkey) enter our brain more easily, sipping on honey before bed—or anytime we feel overwhelmed with stress—can help promote relaxation and restful sleep.

Serves 1

Continued

1 cup water

2 to 3 tablespoons dried peppermint, chamomile, or lemon balm (or another calming herb)

1 to 2 tablespoons honey

1. Bring the water to a boil in a small saucepan. Remove from the heat.

2. Add the herb and allow to steep for 3 for 5 minutes.

3. Strain the tea into a mug, then stir in 1 tablespoon of honey, adding more to taste, as necessary.

Note: If stress is interfering with your daily life or contributing to chronic depression or anxiety, talk to a physician or therapist.

HOT GINGER COLD REMEDY

When my dad was a kid—or so the story goes—my grandfather used to make him a warm concoction of honey, whiskey, and tea to ward off a cold. I recently remembered hearing this tale and thought, *Well, that can't be right—that "remedy" is basically a hot toddy. I'm sure my grandfather didn't give a cocktail to my dad as a sick CHILD!* So, I e-mailed him to quell my curiosity and, sure enough, his response: "Yep. He gave it to me and it worked." As I thought about it, I realized my grandfather was sort of onto something. Honey inhibits the growth of microbes that cause infection and also contains antiviral properties, the steam from a warm beverage helps open sinuses, and—believe it or not—alcohol dilates blood vessels just enough to make it easier for mucous membranes to deal with an infection. It makes sense! Well, except for the whole contributing-to-the-delinquency-of-a-minor thing, but we'll just chalk that up to a different time. This recipe is a great way to soothe and suppress cold symptoms. The addition of warming ginger to the age-old concoction brings a potent anti-inflammatory that helps ease symptoms. And the whiskey is optional, of course, but it's *technically* medicinal and isn't everyone always saying you should "drink plenty of fluids" when you're sick . . . ?

Makes 1 treatment

Continued

1 cup water

One 1-inch piece fresh ginger, grated, minced, or thinly sliced

1 tablespoon fresh lemon juice

1 tablespoon honey

1½ ounces whiskey (optional)

1. Bring the water to a boil in a small saucepan over high heat. Add the ginger, remove from the heat, and allow to steep for 3 to 5 minutes.

2. Meanwhile, place the lemon juice and honey in a mug. Strain the ginger tea into the mug and stir well to combine. Add the shot of whiskey, if you like.

SORE THROAT SOOTHER

Honey all on its own is a very effective sore throat remedy, because it's antibacterial and it acts as a hypertonic osmotic, which is science-speak for something that draws water out of inflamed tissue. So, coating a sore, irritated throat with honey reduces swelling and discomfort. You could easily find relief by just downing a spoonful of honey, but there's something especially soothing about sipping something warm when you're under the weather. No matter the cause of your sore throat—from illness to dry weather to screaming at your favorite sporting event (no judgment here!)—this very simple remedy will have you feeling better in no time.

Makes 1 treatment

2 to 3 teaspoons honey

1 cup hot water or brewed herbal tea

1. Combine the honey and warm liquid in a mug. Stir to combine.

2. Sip slowly.

COUGH SYRUP

Here's something cool: In a double-blind study published in the *Archives of Pediatrics & Adolescent Medicine*, researchers found that buckwheat honey worked better than dextromethorphan (a cough suppressant found in lots of over-the-counter cough syrups) at reducing the frequency and severity of coughing episodes for children. Want to know what's even cooler? The kids weren't the only ones who slept better; the study found that their parents did, too! *Sign me up!*

Why buckwheat honey? The dark, strongly flavored honey is rich in antioxidants as well as antibacterial and antiviral substances that promote healing—and not just in kids. The olive oil soothes and coats, helping everything slide down. This remedy is good for any annoying cough, be the cougher young or old. And by the way, buckwheat is not wheat, it is a completely different botanical species called *Fagopyrum esculentum*, so if you're gluten-free or Paleo or otherwise wheat-averse, don't worry. And if you happen not to have buckwheat honey on hand—though I do recommend tracking some down—making this remedy with another good raw honey will help ease your cough.

Makes about 1 cup

¾ cup buckwheat honey or other raw honey
¼ cup extra-virgin olive oil
Juice of 3 lemons (about ⅓ cup)

1. Place all the ingredients in a glass jar or bottle. Shake or stir to combine. Store in the refrigerator for 4 to 6 weeks or on the counter for up to 2 weeks.

2. To use: Simply give a spoonful as often as needed to soothe coughing (1 to 2 spoonfuls per hour, as necessary).

Important note: Pediatricians recommend waiting until babies are at least 12 months old before feeding them honey because it can contain bacteria that can cause botulism. These bacteria are harmless to adults and children over the age of one, but they can make babies, whose digestive and immune systems are still immature, very sick.

HERBAL COUGH DROPS

Whether it's allergy season or you've managed to pick up a cold or the flu, a sore throat is an unfortunate inevitability for us all—at some point, anyway. Cough drops are one of the sources of relief you may find yourself reaching for at the drugstore. But have you ever taken a good, hard look at the selection in your pharmacy? I mean really *looked* at the ingredient list on the back of all those cough drop packages? They're mostly full of artificial sweeteners, dyes, and tons of other weird, unpronounceable additives. I just can't. Fortunately, making an all-natural cough drop that actually works and is safe for just about everyone in the family (at least those who can manage a cough drop) is totally doable. This recipe features honey, of course, but also relies on slippery elm powder, a natural product made from a type of tree bark that not only soothes, but contains a substance called mucilage that becomes gel-like when combined with water or honey and results in a hard lozenge that requires no cooking at all! This is great news because, if you've ever tried to make candy with honey, you how easily it burns—it's nearly impossible not to end up with a bitter-tasting, scorched mess. This recipe is quick and easy to put together, but does require a long curing time—*at least* a day, so factor that in when making it. If you want to shave some hours off that time, you can dry out the lozenges in a 200°F oven or a dehydrator for a few hours.

Makes about 36 cough drops

1 cup slippery elm powder

4 to 6 tablespoons honey

1 teaspoon ground cinnamon

10 drops orange extract

6 drops lemon extract

1. Place the slippery elm powder, 4 tablespoons of the honey, and the cinnamon in a medium bowl. Stir to combine. You should end up with something resembling soft dough. If the mixture is dry and crumbly, you can add up to 2 more tablespoons of honey to make it easier to work with. The mixture should resemble raw cookie dough.

2. Add the extracts and mix thoroughly until incorporated evenly into the dough.

3. Roll ½-teaspoon-size pieces of the dough into small balls. Place these on parchment-lined baking sheet and leave on the counter, undisturbed, for at least 24 hours, until dry and hard.

4. To store the lozenges, wrap them in waxed paper or store them in an airtight jar.

Note: These are not the glassy-smooth, candylike cough drops you remember from childhood. The texture is more granular, almost sandy, which may take some getting used to, but when these bad boys temper your fury of a sore throat, you'll be sold. Trust me.

SEASONAL ALLERGY FIGHTER

After a long winter, there's a lot to celebrate when spring finally arrives: better weather, beautiful blooming flowers and trees, lighter clothes, radishes, peas, rhubarb . . . But for some (nearly 50 million Americans, to be exact), all that freshness triggers sneezing, wheezing, scratchy throats, and swollen, itching eyes, thanks to tons of pollen floating around all over the place! Aren't allergies just the *worst*?

Some physicians end up prescribing immunotherapy ("allergy shots") for patients with really severe allergies, whereby small amounts of an allergen are administered via injection, typically a couple of times a month for a few years, gradually increasing patients' exposure so as to help their immune system adapt and become less reactive to the triggers. Kind of like a vaccine. Sooooo . . . on the notion that regular exposure to low levels of allergy-triggering pollen is how immunotherapy strengthens a patient's immune system, and on the notion that local honey is full of that very same pollen, wouldn't it make sense to just eat some honey with local pollen in it, to achieve the same effect? Seems pretty logical, which is why local honey is one of the most popular and oldest holistic tricks in the book. Just be sure the honey you're buying is indeed local, and ideally collected from within 50 miles of where you live.

Makes 1 treatment

1 to 2 tablespoons raw, local honey

Take 1 tablespoon of local honey per day for several months prior to allergy season, then 2 tablespoons per day during allergy season. You can eat it straight off the spoon! Of course, spreading it on toast, stirring it into yogurt, and drizzling it on granola are all perfectly acceptable and, perhaps, more civilized methods of intake.

BURN TREATMENT

If you spend as much time in the kitchen as I do, dancing the cha-cha with hot pans, hot ovens, boiling water, and sputtering fat, I'm afraid you'll have occasion to test out your fair share of burn treatments. In my previous books, I've told you about the wonders of apple cider vinegar and baking soda for soothing painful, angry burns and maintain that they're legit treatments—but truth be told, honey is my favorite burn remedy. It soothes and promotes healing better and faster than anything I've tried—and that includes over-the-counter medicines. But don't take my word for it—numerous medical studies, conducted by *actual* doctors and *genuine* scientists, have shown that honey's antibacterial and anti-inflammatory properties make it an enormously effective treatment for burns! In fact, honey is even used in hospital burn units to treat patients with serious burns. *Because it works.* The treatment here is for minor, superficial burns from fire, hot liquids, steam, or sun. If you have been burned severely, seek immediate medical care; emergency treatment can prevent dehydration, shock and/or infection.

Makes 1 treatment

Honey—manuka honey may be especially effective, but any raw honey can be used

Gauze pad

Medical adhesive tape

1. Immediately run the affected area under cold running water for at least 10 minutes.

2. Gently spread a thick layer of honey over the entire burned area.

3. Cover the burn completely with a gauze pad and use medical adhesive tape to secure it in place.

4. Change the bandage daily, applying more honey each time you change the dressing.

Note: A first-degree burn should heal within a week. A small second-degree burn should heal within 2 weeks. If a burn is taking longer than 2 weeks to heal, see your doctor to have the burn checked. Seek immediate medical attention for electrical, chemical, and radiation burns—these should not be treated at home.

ANTISEPTIC FOR CUTS AND SCRAPES

Using honey to help wounds heal is not exactly newfangled medicine. People have been slathering it on their boo-boos since Egyptian doctors first recorded its ability to heal skin circa 2000 BCE. With tons of antioxidants, amino acids, vitamins, and minerals, honey fights bacteria that infect wounds, thanks in part to an enzyme called glucose oxidase, excreted by worker bees, which releases low levels of hydrogen peroxide when the honey makes contact with a wound. Plus, its thick, gooey texture allows a cut to heal in a moist environment, which can help minimize scarring. And under the heading of "Things That Are Kind of Gross but Also Sort of Cool" is the fact that when honey is applied to wounded tissue, a chemical reaction takes place that makes it smell good. So, um, there's that. Most minor cuts or scrapes are harmless and will go away after a few days, but since they *can* sometimes become infected, it's always a good idea to keep them clean and promote healing. Here's how to treat *minor* cuts and scrapes:

Makes 1 treatment

Honey

Gauze pad

Waterproof adhesive bandage

1. Wash the wound with clean water.

2. Apply a thin layer of honey to a gauze pad and place directly on top of the wound.

3. Cover the pad with a larger, waterproof adhesive bandage.

4. Change the dressing daily, until the injury is completely healed.

DIGESTIVE AID

A churning stomach—whether from nerves or from food (too much, too little, simply the wrong ones—I'm looking at you, raw onions)—is no party at all. However, adding honey to a tummy gone wrong can definitely help to turn things around. The soothing properties of honey relieve acidity in the stomach and improve digestion. It also defuses gas, making it an excellent antidote for overeating. If you've overindulged or are otherwise having a rough time in your tummy, give this gingery honey remedy a try.

Makes 1 treatment

1 tablespoon grated fresh ginger

1 tablespoon fresh lemon juice

2 tablespoons honey

1 cup warm water

Combine all the ingredients in a glass or mug. Stir well. Sip slowly.

DANDRUFF SOLUTION

If you've ever had dandruff, you know that getting rid of it is no easy task. Contrary to popular belief, dandruff doesn't come from having a dry scalp. The cause is still slightly unclear, but dermatologists generally believe it's a response to natural yeast that's found on the skin, and it tends to flare up with stress and cold, dry weather. A whole world of dandruff treatments out there promise to rid your scalp of its trademark dry, scaly, even waxy flakes, but most over-the-counter dandruff products are full of chemicals and scary-sounding medications.

For a natural approach that works wonders on frustrating flakes, take that trusty jar of honey into the shower with you. Research has shown that raw honey can treat even severe dandruff problems. Credit goes to honey's antimicrobial properties, which block the yeast that causes dandruff. Before you try yet another medicated shampoo, give this sweet remedy a shot.

Makes 1 treatment

6 tablespoons raw honey
2 tablespoons warm water

1. Mix the honey and water in a small bowl or squeeze bottle.

2. Apply directly to the hair and massage it into the scalp for a few minutes.

3. Leave it on for a few hours—for long hair, you may want to

wear a shower cap to catch drips—then rinse thoroughly with warm water.

4. Repeat every other day for 2 weeks, then once a week for maintenance.

HANGOVER HELPER

Okay, so you had one too many. Last night was fun and all, but today you're a foggy, nauseated pile of headache and remorse. It happens. And while we've all got our go-to hangover cures (Alka-Seltzer? Pickle juice? A little "hair of the dog"? Greasy takeout and reality TV?), what science suggests, aside from time and plenty of water, is to take in some honey to deal with the toxic effects of overindulging.

According to the Royal Society of Chemistry, the fructose in honey helps the body metabolize alcohol, plus it contains potassium, which is depleted when you drink too much and needs to be replaced the morning after. Ingest honey by itself or, better yet, give this yummy honey toast a try. Because, you gotta eat, right? Surely you know how to make toast, even when you're not firing on all cylinders—so consider this less of a recipe and more of a friendly reminder to take care of yourself. Feel better!

Serves 1

1 slice good bread, such as sourdough, hearty whole wheat, or multigrain

Butter (optional—but, really, is it?)

1 teaspoon honey, Creamed Honey (page 90), or Whipped Honey Butter (page 88), or more to taste

Pinch of sea salt (optional)

1. Toast the bread in a toaster or under your oven's broiler for 2 to 4 minutes, until it is toasted to your liking.

2. Spread butter (if using) on the toast, then drizzle with the honey and sprinkle with salt.

NATURAL SLEEP AID

Getting enough sleep isn't easy. From time changes to anxieties to nighttime distractions (read: *put down your phone!*), getting some shut-eye is often harder than we'd like it to be. Research has shown that adequate sleep can support our metabolism, stabilize our hormones, and boost our mood. Without it, not only are we looking at low energy and bleariness, but also potentially serious health consequences, such as increased cortisol (the stress hormone) levels, and higher risk for hypertension, obesity, type 2 diabetes, heart disease, stroke, and arthritis.

Sure, some people can function on less sleep than others (maybe parents of small infants and—oh, I don't know—superheroes like Oprah?), but in general, we should all be getting somewhere between seven and nine hours of zzz's a night. Good news for those of us struggling to hit those numbers: honey has been a popular sleep-inducing remedy for thousands of years. When taken before bed, honey actually stabilizes blood sugar levels, supports our liver in detoxification and circulation, and contributes to the release of melatonin—an important sleep hormone.

Makes 1 treatment

2 teaspoons apple cider vinegar
2 teaspoons honey
1 cup warm water

1. Before bedtime, stir the vinegar and honey into a cup of warm water.

2. Drink while warm.

3. Good night.

ENERGY-BOOSTING TONIC

It doesn't matter who we are—a student, an athlete, a desk jockey—we all hit that dreaded three o'clock slump sometimes. You know it when it happens: your energy takes a nosedive, killing your motivation to do anything that resembles productivity. Coffee and caffeinated soda are popular quick fixes, but they have some serious downsides, such as sugar and/or chemical sweeteners and the inevitable crash that comes after the buzz. Fortunately, there is a better way! Honey! It's a great source of carbohydrates and a natural energy booster. With a unique nutritional composition, antioxidants, enzymes, minerals, vitamins, and amino acids, honey is a natural energy-filled source of nutrition. In fact, many athletes include pure honey into their pre-exercise meal or snack for that very reason. With no refined sugar, no artificial colors (*Why* are there so many blue drinks out there?!), and no caffeine, this drink is simply all-natural deliciousness that just so happens to promote quick fluid absorption for hydration and quality carbohydrate energy for working muscles. So, the next time you find yourself in an afternoon slump, give this energizing tonic a try. Then, watch out, to-do list!

Serves 2

2 cups coconut water

Juice of 2 limes

Juice of 1 lemon

⅛ teaspoon sea salt

1 tablespoon raw honey

1. Combine the coconut water, lime and lemon juice, salt, and honey in a blender. Blend until the honey dissolves.

2. Drink immediately, or store in an airtight jar in the fridge for up to 3 days.

MANUKA HONEY PLAQUE REDUCER

You know the old saying: "Some honey a day keeps the dentist away." Wait. What? Of course not! We all know that too much sweet stuff is *bad* for your teeth and gums. It rots your teeth and causes cavities! So, using honey as part of your daily dental hygiene would be crazy, right? Wait. What? Okay, here's a mind-blower for you: Manuka honey, which we already know is more or less magical fairy dust in liquid form, is effective in treating gum disease and preventing tooth decay. Yep, it has been shown to curb dental plaque and bacterial growth in the mouth, thanks to a compound called methylglyoxal as well as a host of supercharged antibacterial, antiseptic, and antimicrobial properties. In one major study of manuka's effect on dental health, researchers discovered that using manuka honey not only caused a 35 percent decrease in plaque, but it led to a 35 percent reduction in bleeding gums in people who suffered from gingivitis. All of which is to say that using manuka honey is a pretty sweet way to improve your dental health. (Wink.) Here's a very simple method for incorporating it into your daily routine.

Makes 1 treatment

½ teaspoon manuka honey

1 to 2 ounces room-temperature water (filtered or tap)

1. Combine the honey and water in a small cup.

2. After brushing, swish the solution around in your mouth, as you would any other mouthwash, for about 30 seconds, then spit it out.

3. Use daily.

Note: Manuka honey is seriously pricey stuff, so you'll want to use it sparingly. You'll also want to make sure you're getting the real deal. If it's authentic manuka honey, it will have a UMF quality trademark on its label, noting that it has been packaged in New Zealand and tested for purity. If not, buyer beware!

PINKEYE REMEDY

In summer, when my family heads to the pool several days a week, you'd think my mom brain would be mostly focused on remembering plenty of towels, snacks, water, and sunscreen so we can all enjoy this relaxed, carefree, fun time of year. You'd think. But would you like to know what my mom brain is actually focused on (while simultaneously packing up pretzels, towels, sunscreen, and dry clothes)? Pinkeye. I think my kids had it *at least* four times last summer. And while I'm not 100 percent sure where it came from, I'd be willing to bet my beautiful red stand mixer that the pool did it. Pinkeye: an inflammatory condition that can be viral, bacterial, or allergy-related, affects the conjunctiva (the thin membrane that covers the eye). When this membrane becomes irritated or inflamed, the blood vessels enlarge, the eye goes red and—if you're "lucky"—oozes pus. It's horrid. Oh, and it's crazy contagious, which is especially awesome if your kids get it and you're an adult who likes to wear mascara and do stuff like *be seen in public*!

So, what's a busy mom to do when she herself gets hit with this nasty plague that threatens to send the household ecosystem into utter imbalance? Put honey on her eyeball, obviously. I mean . . . if honey is so great at healing wounds, preventing cavities, soothing burns, and killing infection, it must be able to do *something* for a raging case of pinkeye, right? A little Internet sleuthing confirmed it: honey is commonly used to treat various kinds of eye irritation and has been for millennia. So it's settled, then. Honey in the eye. This recipe, based on an old home remedy, makes more drops than you'll ever need. (I hope!) Use the treatment until you feel better, then toss the leftovers.

Makes 1 treatment

¼ teaspoon raw honey

¼ cup distilled water (or water that has been boiled for 5 minutes and allowed to cool)

1. Dissolve raw honey in warm (not hot) water in a sterile jar.

2. Using a *clean* dropper, place 1 to 2 drops in each eye every few hours, as needed.

Note: Most cases of pinkeye are mild and get better without treatment. If you experience severe pain, blurred vision, or symptoms that don't improve after a day or two, you should see your health care provider. And a baby with pinkeye symptoms should always be seen by a doctor.

PART FOUR

HONEY FOR
BEAUTY

HONEY FACIAL SCRUB

A great exfoliating face wash makes all the difference in the world. And I know because, over the years, I have *more* than done my part to keep the skincare industry in business. The problem, though, with so many of the fancy face scrubs I used to buy (and buy and buy) is that while they smelled nice and may have made my skin look good, they were really expensive and—worse—often contained plastics, irritating fragrances, glycerin, parabens, phthalates, and other dubious ingredients.

A few years ago, after trying—and failing—to decode the ingredient list on a super-high-end sugar scrub I was using, I decided to try my hand at making my own. I figured there couldn't be much more than sugar in a good sugar scrub! This recipe is the result. With nothing more than brown sugar (a gentle exfoliant and source of bacteria-fighting glycolic acid) and honey (a natural humectant and bacteria zapper), this scrub smooths, buffs, and draws moisture to the skin, leaving it soft and supple. Use it once or twice a week to keep your complexion clear and your skin looking healthy.

Makes 1 treatment

1 tablespoon raw honey
1 tablespoon light brown sugar

Combine the honey and sugar in the palm of your hand. Massage into clean, damp skin in a circular motion. Rinse thoroughly with warm water. Pat dry.

CUCUMBER HONEY TONER

I have to confess that I've misjudged toner over the years. I think that because my initial introduction to it was as a teenager using a popular blue-tinted "astringent," my assumption was always that toner was supposed to be a *super* harsh, this-stings-so-it-must-be-working kind of thing. Not the case, actually. Think of toner as the dental floss of the skincare world. Yes, a good face cleanser is important, just like brushing with toothpaste is the backbone of good oral hygiene, but you aren't really done cleaning your mouth until you floss away all the gunk your toothbrush can't reach. Same with toner—you really haven't finished washing your face until you use toner to clear your pores of whatever remaining residue and impurities your cleanser missed. Plus, toner helps balance your skin's pH (i.e., how acidic it is), which goes a little off after washing. This easy DIY toner recipe is perfect for calming, balancing, and cleansing skin. The cucumber soothes and softens because it has the same pH as healthy skin, and the honey helps maintain moisture. Use it regularly, and you'll be armed against dry skin, a puffy face, blemishes, and other assorted skin blahs.

Makes about ½ cup

1 medium cucumber, peeled and roughly chopped
2 teaspoons honey

1. Place the cucumber chunks in a blender and process until smooth.

2. Strain the cucumber puree through a cheesecloth-lined sieve (you can also use a paper coffee filter), allowing all the juice to collect in a glass bowl or measuring cup. Give it about 15 to 20 minutes.

3. Pour the cucumber juice into a clean glass bottle or jar and add the honey. Shake well to combine. Refrigerate for up to 1 month.

4. To use, shake the bottle and saturate a cotton pad or two with the toner. Sweep over your clean face, neck, and décolletage. Continue with your regular skincare routine.

ZIT ZAPPER

There's a lot I don't miss about being a teenager: algebra, questionable haircuts, general social awkwardness, and, of course—clichéd as it may be—pimples. While I never had *severe* acne (just severely bad hair), I always depended on my trusty tube of thick, white, harsh, and drying zit cream to get me through occasional breakouts. Fast-forward a few years and guess what? I *still* have to contend with the occasional pimple, even now that I'm (supposedly) a grown-up. Suffice it to say, I've had a long time to test out all kinds of treatments and can tell you that my favorite at-home remedy for acne is green tea and honey. Green tea is a natural anti-inflammatory and can decrease redness and swelling, while honey—an antibacterial, as we know—can destroy acne-causing germs. This remedy is quick, easy, and really mild (yet effective), making it safe for all skin types, even sensitive skin. And, most important, it'll zap any zit that dares to show up.

Makes 1 treatment

1 tea bag green tea
8 ounces boiling water
1 teaspoon honey

1. Place the tea bag in the hot water and allow to steep for 5 minutes.

2. Add the honey and stir to dissolve. Allow the mixture to cool completely.

3. Once cooled, soak a cotton ball in the liquid and apply it to the pimple for at least 1 minute. Allow to dry.

BRIGHTENING AND TIGHTENING FACIAL MASK

Here's a spa-quality treatment to make at home that will exfoliate, brighten, and moisturize your skin—no appointment necessary! It's potent yet gentle enough for most complexions, and super easy to (literally) whip up. The ingredient list may look wacky (I know, I know, mayonnaise seems weird), but trust me on this one. It works! The vitamin C and alpha hydroxy acids in the strawberries and the naturally grainy bee pollen granules exfoliate the skin, helping the honey, which we know is a potent humectant, to better penetrate and work its magic. Olive oil is a fantastic moisturizer and is infused with antioxidants. Mayonnaise is rich in omega-3 and -6 fatty acids that repair damaged skin and promote cell regeneration and it gives a hit of vitamin A, vitamin K, and proteins that improve skin's elasticity. And as for the essential oil? Well, that's because . . . mayonnaise.

Makes 1 treatment

3 strawberries, mashed

2 tablespoons bee pollen granules

2 tablespoons honey

1 teaspoon olive oil

2 teaspoons store-bought mayonnaise

2 to 3 drops of essential oil, such as lavender, rose, or lemon

Continued

1. Place all the ingredients in a small bowl. Whisk to combine.

2. Apply the mixture to a just-cleaned face, avoiding the eye area. Relax for 20 minutes, then rinse with warm water.

HOMEMADE LIP BALM

Surprisingly quick and staggeringly easy to make, this stuff is *da* balm! With ingredients that moisturize and protect, this balm is not only as effective for soothing and preventing chapped lips as any ready-made lip balm you might grab at the checkout line at the grocery store—if not more so—but it's 100 percent natural and much less expensive. The shea butter and coconut oil offer a silky, smooth texture that glides on like a dream. The added honey makes it ever so slightly sweet and extra moisturizing and the peppermint oil gives it a fun, cooling sensation. And speaking of oils, this recipe is completely customizable, so . . . say, you don't like peppermint? No problemo! Use something else, such as lavender, vanilla, orange, or *chocolate* (gasp!). You can even get creative and add color or shimmer (see note) to your lip balm, which, of course, absolutely screams "gift giving." If you want, you can even decorate the pots or tubes with cute labels, a bit of paper or some fun washi tape, and then all that's left to do is open your own Etsy shop.

Makes 10 to 12 pots or tubes

3 tablespoons coconut oil

1 tablespoon beeswax pellets

1 teaspoon shea butter or cocoa butter

1 teaspoon honey

6 to 8 drops food-grade peppermint oil

Lip balm tubes or tins

1. Combine the coconut oil, beeswax, and shea butter in a small, heat-safe bowl or mason jar and place into a small saucepan filled with water over medium-low heat, stirring until the mixture is completely melted. Add the honey and stir to incorporate.

2. Remove from the heat and stir in the peppermint oil, then carefully pour into tubes or tins and let set for at least 1 hour.

3. Store in a cool, dry place.

Note: To add color to homemade lip balm, add a bit of lipstick to your wax and oils as they are melting—just scrape a bit off the end of the lipstick. The more you add, the more intense your hue will be. Stir well for even color. And if you (or your kids) want to add a touch of sparkle—use edible glitter! Yep, from the baking aisle of your local craft store.

LIP SCRUB

On a recent morning, as I was standing outside in front of our compost pile, I started to wonder whether there was something amazing, useful, and cool I could be doing with the morning's spent coffee grounds as I was about to add them to our growing pile of kitchen scraps. Curious, I brought them back inside and then it took all of about half a second of Googling to find out that there are about a bazillion amazing, useful, and cool things one can do with old coffee grounds. Where had *I* been?! Turns out you can use coffee grounds to repel slugs in the garden, scour pots and pans, mask furniture scratches and remove onion smell from your hands—to name but a few. My favorite discovery, however, is this awesome lip scrub. With just three products from your kitchen cupboard—coffee grounds, olive oil, and honey—you can make a great scrub in less than five minutes. And lest you think that scrubbing your lips is a completely ridiculous and unnecessary step in a beauty routine that already asks more of you than you have to give (as I did), let me just say this: to really, effectively moisturize dry, chapped lips, you have to get rid of the old, cracked, dead skin cells before you slather on lip balm. Otherwise, the moisture can't get where it needs to go; it's blocked by a barrier of blech. You'll especially love this stuff when winter rolls around, and you're desperate for some moisture and softness. Use once or twice a week to remove flakes and soften and polish your pout.

Makes 2 or 3 treatments

2 tablespoons used coffee grounds

1 teaspoon honey

½ teaspoon olive oil

1. Combine all the ingredients in a small bowl or jar, stirring until well blended.

2. Use your finger to apply some of the mixture to your lips and, using a circular motion, scrub for up to 1 minute.

3. Rinse off with water and pat dry.

CONDITIONING HAIR TREATMENT

Hair coloring, heat styling, sun, and dry weather, even your hair's natural texture—especially if it's curly—can leave you with dry and/or damaged hair. With my own head of curly, tending-toward-dry hair, I've invested significant time and serious cash searching high and low, near and far, in drugstores, salons, health food stores, and online for the best hydrating hair products. Of course, when it comes to DIY hair treatments, this ain't my first rodeo. Believe me, there isn't much I won't dump on my head in the name of hair hydration—bananas, eggs, olive oil, mayonnaise, coconut oil, beer . . . I've tried them all to see which, if any, could turn my parched hair into the soft and shiny tresses of my dreams. The problem with a lot of those homemade treatments is that they tend to leave my hair greasy or limp or both. Not exactly what I'm going for. But this honey treatment? This one is different. First of all, there's no oil to speak of, so you won't end up with hair that is weighed down or dirty-looking, which can happen after an oily treatment. Plus it combines just two natural ingredients—honey and yogurt—both of which are incredibly nourishing, hydrating, and emollient. And my favorite part? If you're running late in the morning, you can make a double batch and eat half for breakfast. I'm (half) kidding!

Makes 1 treatment

2 tablespoons plain, whole-milk yogurt (or more for longer
  hair)

1 tablespoon honey (or more for longer hair)

1. Combine the yogurt and honey in a small bowl.

2. Work the mixture onto your hair, from roots to ends, massaging the mask into your scalp.

3. Leave the mixture on your hair for 15 to 20 minutes, covered with a plastic shower cap if you like, before rinsing
   thoroughly.

4. Use this treatment once a week to restore and maintain
   your hair.

THE PERFECT SHOWER GEL

If asked to describe the difference between taking a bath and taking a shower, I'd be willing to bet that most people would characterize baths as indulgent and relaxing and showers as more or less compulsory. And, while it's true that there's something intrinsically soothing about soaking in a warm tub, especially one that's scented with something lovely like lavender, a shower can be restorative and calming, too—*if* you're using the right stuff. This homemade body wash is not only good for your skin, with gently cleansing Castile soap, emollient oils, and nourishing honey, it smells freaking fantastic and feels super luxe on your skin. Because there are no weird chemical emulsifiers in there, you may find that it separates a bit in the shower. This isn't a problem. Just give the bottle a good shake before you use it, then take a deep breath in. Smell that? That's the sweet, sweet scent of the *perfect* shower gel.

Makes about 1 cup

⅔ cup unscented liquid Castile soap

¼ cup honey

2 teaspoons jojoba, almond, or untoasted sesame oil

1 teaspoon vitamin E oil

50 to 60 drops essential oil (see note)

1. Combine all the ingredients in a bottle with a squirt top or a pump, shaking to mix.

2. To use, shake well, then squirt onto a washcloth or directly onto your body.

A few words on fragrance: The sky's the limit when it comes to scenting your shower gel. Any combination of essential oils will work here—use one, use a few—just be sure to use scents you really love and you can't go wrong. If you're looking for ideas, here are a few that I happen to like, listed with some of their skin benefits:

Geranium: Great for oily skin, acne, dull skin, eczema.
Grapefruit: Tones and cleanses.
Lavender: Good for all skin types. Soothing scent.
Patchouli: Antimicrobial, astringent, beneficial for cracked and chapped skin.
Rosemary: Stimulating and restorative. Good for acne, eczema, and dermatitis.
Sandalwood: Great for all skin types, especially mature skin.
Sweet orange: Brightening and revitalizing.
Tea tree: Antibacterial; highly therapeutic for acne and inflamed skin.
Vanilla: Antibacterial. Great for general skin care.

MOISTURIZING LOTION BARS

Lotion bars have been kind of a revelation in my house and I'll tell you one of the reasons: Have you ever witnessed the horror show that is a tube of lotion in the hands of a toddler? The aftermath looks like a crime scene after the murders of many, many marshmallows. Lotion bars are solid, like a bar of soap, so there's no squeezing involved, which makes them not only toddlerproof, but also perfect for traveling, gift giving, and everyday use. They're solid at room temperature—thanks to honey's superstar cousin, beeswax—but the warmth of your skin softens and melts the bars, so to use them, all you have to do is rub one over the surface you want to moisturize, and voilà—you've got lotion where you need it. I love these bars in winter when my hands are raw and cracked from the cold, dry air. I keep one in my handbag, one on my nightstand, and one at the kitchen sink. In summer, I stash one in the pool bag to use as an after-sun soother. You can certainly get fancy with these, using cute molds or adding fragrance, spices, or shimmer (see lip balm notes, page 153), but the truth is, you really can keep it simple and still end up with a fabulous moisturizer. I've made these bars in muffin tins and ice cube trays, both of which work perfectly well. You can even spray the sides of a loaf pan with nonstick spray and then cut slices for individual use.

Makes about 1 cup; number of bars depends on mold size

Continued

BASIC LOTION BAR:

⅓ cup coconut oil

⅓ cup shea butter or cocoa butter

⅓ cup beeswax

1. Combine the coconut oil, shea butter, and beeswax in a small, heat-safe bowl or mason jar and place in a small saucepan filled with water over medium-low heat, stirring until the mixture is completely melted.

2. Pour the melted ingredients into molds.

3. Set aside and allow to cool, about 30 minutes to an hour, until solid.

4. Remove the bars from the molds and store away from direct sunlight and direct heat for up to a year.

Lavender Lotion Bars:

Stir 10 drops of lavender essential oil and 1 tablespoon of dried lavender buds into the melted ingredients, then proceed with the recipe.

Bronzing Lotion Bars:

Stir 1 tablespoon of bronze mica powder, 1 teaspoon of unsweetened cocoa powder, and ½ teaspoon of ground cinnamon into the melted ingredients, then proceed with the recipe.

Sore Muscle Treatment Bars:

Stir ½ teaspoon of ground cayenne pepper, 1 tablespoon of menthol crystals, and 10 drops of peppermint or wintergreen essential oil into the melted ingredients, then proceed with the recipe.

MILK AND HONEY ELBOW SOFTENER

So, you've got yourself some dry elbows. Well, guess what? You aren't alone. Dry, flaky, even cracked elbows are not only annoying, but fairly common. See, the skin on your elbow is quite different from the skin on other parts of your body. It tends to be *much* thicker and, because there are fewer oil-secreting glands there, it's drier than other parts. And here I thought having thick skin was a good thing! Actually it is—since elbow skin is so thick, it's able to withstand all the stretching, bending, and friction it endures day in and day out, which is great and all, and let's all be grateful for our working parts, but *still*! Rough, darkened, leathery elbows stink, especially if you're rocking a sleeveless look. Here's a treatment to use on those unsightly suckers that combines soothing, hydrating honey with milk—a source of lactic acid that exfoliates, lightens, and brightens skin. Use it daily, and you'll see smoother, softer elbows before you know it!

Makes 1 treatment

½ cup milk

2 tablespoons honey

1. Stir the milk and honey together in a small bowl.

2. Massage the mixture into your elbows and allow it to penetrate the skin for 5 to 10 minutes.

3. Rinse thoroughly, pat dry, and follow with a thick moisturizing cream.

SKIN-SOFTENING HONEY BATH

Quick literary quiz: Who was Shakespeare talking about when he wrote, "Age cannot wither her"? I'll give you a hint: she was a legendarily beautiful Egyptian queen, famous for her über-trendy winged eyeliner, who captured the hearts of both Julius Caesar and Mark Antony. Did you guess Elizabeth Taylor? Ohhhh, *so close*! The answer, of course, is Cleopatra. Renowned for her radiance, she famously bathed in milk and honey. (Apparently, she used donkey's milk, but no need for us to dwell on that detail. *Move along, move along.*)

And now you, too, can give your skin the royal treatment with this luxurious bath—using milk (which contains exfoliating lactic acid), and honey (which softens, hydrates, and all-around pampers). For a decadent bath that will not only rejuvenate your skin but also give you a mini escape from the stress of daily life, give this a try.

Makes 1 bath

2 to 3 cups whole milk, or 1 cup powdered whole milk

½ cup honey

¼ cup almond oil (optional)

1. Pour the milk, honey, and almond oil (if using) into your bath water as you're filling the tub.

2. Lie back, relax, and enjoy a luxurious soak, Your Majesty.

HONEY MINT MOUTHWASH

I don't want to freak you out or anything, but I thought you should know: your mouth is *full* of bacteria—millions and millions of bacteria, good and bad. If you're wondering whether that's what accounts for stinky breath, then *ding-ding*—you are correcto! Bacteria like to eat, and when they're done, they have to get rid of their waste, if you know what I mean. Hydrogen sulfide. *That* is what stinks, and *that* is what signals us to grab for that bottle of mouthwash. The thing is, commercial mouthwash is full of alcohol, which, yes, kills bacteria, but can actually alter the natural pH of the mouth. It also contains detergents, fake sugars (e.g., sorbitol and saccharin), synthetic colors (*why* is it blue?), and artificial fragrance and flavorings—all of which mess with the natural flora in your mouth. The good news is that making your own all-natural mouthwash is incredibly easy, as in five ingredients easy. Of course, one of those ingredients is honey, which contrary to what you may be thinking, does *not* promote tooth decay. Just the opposite, thank you very much! Here, honey not only makes this mouthwash taste sweet, but it also helps kill the bad bacteria that are giving you dragon breath.

Makes 2 cups

1 cup warm distilled or filtered water

1 tablespoon honey

Juice of ½ lemon

5 drops food-grade spearmint oil

5 drops food-grade peppermint oil

5 drops food-grade anise or clove oil

1. Combine all the ingredients in a glass bottle or jar. Stir or shake well. Store in a cool, dark place.

2. To use: shake well, then swish around in your mouth and/or gargle for 1 to 2 minutes. Spit, rinse, and enjoy fresh breath.

PART FIVE

MIND YOUR BEESWAX (HOUSEHOLD USES FOR HONEY AND BEESWAX)

RUST PREVENTER

You know that thing where you start out your online travels by looking up showtimes at your local movie theater and somehow, an hour later, end up deep in an exploration of at-home blacksmithing? That has *literally* happened to me, which is how I learned all about using beeswax as a rust preventer. It is also how I learned that you can DIY a forge out of an old coffee can, ceramic wool, and a propane torch. (But, don't worry, I haven't tried it. Yet.) While most of us may not be forging our own iron tools or even thinking too much about the potential for rust on the undercarriage of our cars (another place where it turns out beeswax can be useful), we all have plenty around the house—from cast-iron cookware to shovels, nails, screws, and tools—that has the potential to rust if we don't stay on top of things. To add protection and longevity to your metal objects, follow this simple method.

Beeswax (solid or pastilles)

1. Place the beeswax in a heat-safe bowl. Set the bowl over a saucepan filled with 1 inch of boiling water over medium heat (think: double boiler). Stir occasionally. Once melted, remove from the heat and allow the beeswax to cool slightly.

2. Using a soft cloth or chamois, rub a thin layer of the melted wax over the surface of the metal you want to protect. Allow it to dry, then buff with a clean cloth to remove any excess.

BEESWAX WOOD CONDITIONER AND FURNITURE POLISH

I have a wooden cutting board that I absolutely love. I "inherited" it from some neighbors when they were redoing their kitchen. Right place, right time. Lucky me! It's a true kitchen workhorse, as good cutting boards are—worthy of some extra TLC. My routine for babying my board *used* to be: scrub it down daily with lemon and salt, disinfect it weekly with baking soda, and massage it with a bit of mineral oil whenever it started to look a little sad and dried out. That protocol worked fine, but at some point, I was turned on to this DIY beeswax-based wood conditioner and started using that in place of the straight mineral oil, with superior results. Because I was so pleased with the way it worked on my board, I started using the mixture all over the house and soon realized how indispensable it was! I discovered that it worked well on wooden salad bowls, wooden spoons, wooden toys, and, *by golly*, I thought, *someone who is really good at cleaning their house would LOVE this stuff for polishing furniture!* (I "polish" my furniture with paper towels and spilled apple juice. To each her own.) It restores shine and gloss, improves color, and adds to the character and beauty of wooden pieces. With *two* ingredients! You'll want to be sure to use oil that won't go rancid, because rotten oil is gross. I suggest mineral oil, but you could also use baby oil (which, I'm pretty sure, is the same thing) or fractionated coconut oil.

Makes about 1 cup

¼ cup beeswax

1 cup mineral oil or fractioned coconut oil

1. Combine the beeswax and oil in a heat-safe bowl. Set the bowl over a saucepan filled with 1 inch of boiling water over medium heat (think: double boiler). Stir occasionally. Once the beeswax is melted, remove from the heat and allow the beeswax to cool slightly.

2. Once cooled, the mixture will be thick and creamy. At this point, it can be scooped into a glass jar or other lidded container for storage.

3. To use, apply a liberal amount of the polish onto a wooden surface. Massage and buff with a clean, soft cloth. Leave the wooden item alone for several hours or overnight, then reapply or buff off any leftovers.

Did you know? You can also use beeswax to lubricate squeaky or stuck furniture. Just rub some beeswax on the edges of windows, drawers, or doors that tend to stick, and they'll glide smoothly.

LEATHER CONDITIONER

If you have leather furniture—and even if you don't—you probably think it's difficult to keep it clean, shiny, and supple. Sure, there are commercial leather cleaners out there—even some that come in convenient wipes form—but they're expensive, especially if you have a lot of surface area to clean, their results are usually fairly short-lived, and they're often filled with chemicals that we don't exactly want to be rubbing up against with any regularity. This recipe solves all that and more. It cleans but also conditions, to keep your leather goods—jackets, handbags, shoes, wallets, even the seats in your car—soft, supple, and shiny. And this conditioner lasts a long, long time. The combination of protective beeswax and nourishing oils prevents the leather from drying and cracking, and also keeps outside elements (e.g., salt and dirt) from penetrating and staining the leather. It will work on any kind of leather, but not on suede, which has its own brand of high-maintenance going on.

Makes about 1 cup

¼ cup beeswax
¼ cup cocoa butter or coconut oil
½ cup sweet almond oil

1. Place all the ingredients in a small saucepan and melt over medium heat, stirring occasionally.

2. Pour into a glass jar or small metal tin and allow the mixture to cool until solid, about 30 minutes.

3. To use, apply the conditioner directly to the leather with your fingers or a soft cloth, gently massaging it into the leather. Once finished, wipe away any excess, then buff the leather with a clean cloth to make it shine.

GRANITE COUNTERTOP POLISH

When we decided to move from the city to the suburbs, we looked at a lot of very old homes that we loved, and while the idea of renovating was tempting, some soul-searching led my husband and me to the realization that living through a gut renovation with a then-toddler and infant was likely a recipe for a matching set of his and hers nervous breakdowns. So, we decided we would be "the people who live in the house after the people who fixed the house." Like most things in life, there are pros and cons to this strategy. On the one hand, you get to skip months of construction, constant dust, and considerable inconvenience. On the other hand, you inherit someone else's taste and design choices. In our case, it meant inheriting a great kitchen with a lot of granite. Now, I know granite is pretty ubiquitous in kitchens these days, but I'd never owned it before and wanted to know how to care for it. Here's a tip: if you want to learn about caring for granite, *do not* Internet search "best ways to care for granite." It's *so* confusing, and you'll find yourself muttering things like "Wait, is there anything I *can* use to clean this thing?" Trust me, for daily cleanup, any old multipurpose countertop spray will work. But to keep your counters shiny and to prevent staining and scratching, a good polish and seal with beeswax will keep them looking good as new. Here's how.

Makes 1 treatment

1 cup beeswax pellets (more or less, depending on the size of your countertop)

1. Place the beeswax in a heat-safe bowl. Set the bowl over a saucepan filled with 1 inch of boiling water over medium heat (think: double boiler). Stir occasionally.

2. Once melted, remove from the heat and allow the beeswax to cool for a minute or two, then spread a thin layer on the countertop and allow it to absorb for 10 to 15 minutes. Then, buff it off with a chamois or soft cloth.

ECO-FRIENDLY REUSABLE FOOD WRAP

Hard as I've tried to avoid it, we use a lot of plastic in our house. Sandwich bags, grocery bags, snack bags, garbage bags, plastic wrap, water bottles, food containers . . . *aarrrgh—too much!* I *try* to reuse them, but if I'm being honest . . . I usually don't; they're hard to clean and just generally difficult to reuse. (I mean, they aren't designed to be reused, so I suppose that makes sense.) But then, as I consider the waste and the chemicals and the impact on the environment and the expense, and—if I'm *really* honest—the unattractiveness of all that plastic, well, that's the kind of thinking that once led me to a mild breakdown over it all. "That's it," I said to my family, "I can't handle the plastic anymore!! *Noooo more plastic!*" And I marched right over my computer, geared up to order a few dozen (adorable!) beeswax-coated 100 percent organic cotton reusable food wraps. "*What the what?!* I'm not paying $20 for three stupid pieces of waxed fabric!" And, with that, I resolved to make my own. You won't believe how easy it is to make this natural, reusable alternative to plastic wrap. It creates a watertight seal around your food, so that you can wrap up all manner of sandwiches, snacks, fruits, vegetables, and leftovers. Reduce, reuse, recycle, rewrap.

Fabric (ideally some sort of natural fabric, such as cotton—I like to repurpose old bedsheets and cloth napkins.)

Beeswax (pellets or, if you have solid beeswax, grate it on a box grater)

1. Preheat the oven to 200°F.

2. Cut your fabric to the desired shape and size (you can use pinking shears, if you have them, to prevent the fabric from fraying or—my favorite trick—use old cloth napkins with a finished edge!)

3. Place the fabric is a single layer on a parchment-lined baking sheet. Sprinkle with about a tablespoon of wax pellets or grated beeswax.

4. Put the sheet pan in the oven and heat for 5 minutes, until the wax starts to melt.

5. Using a clean toothbrush or pastry brush, spread the melted wax over the fabric in an even layer. No need to flip the fabric—the wax will saturate it completely.

6. Transfer the beeswax fabric to a clean piece of fabric or towel and allow it to dry.

To use:

Place one of your food wraps over the bowl or container you want to cover and press around the edges. The warmth from your hands will make it pliable enough to hold its shape. To wrap a sandwich, hunk of cheese, piece of fruit, and so on, just fold the wrap around the food item and press the edges together.

Continued

To clean your wraps:

Rinse in cool, mildly soapy water. If necessary, give them a gentle rub with a dishcloth or sponge. Don't use hot water or the beeswax will melt.

IDIOT-PROOF DIY BEESWAX CANDLES

I like to DIY. Not because I am especially artistic or crafty (or good at following directions), but because there is something undeniably satisfying about *making* things. I do confess that not every one of my DIY endeavors has ended in success. Or even in completion, now that I think about it. But then there are the DIY projects that are so easy, so idiot-proof, so awesomely impossible to mess up that you almost can't believe it. This here is one of *those* projects. Jar candles are Easy with a capital *E*. We're talking about your basic melt-and-pour type of operation. Plus, they're attractive, they burn slow and clean (unlike paraffin candles, which release carcinogens into the air), and they make lovely hostess gifts and party favors.

Makes 2 to 6 candles, depending on the size of your jars

Jars, tins, or other nonflammable containers anywhere from 4 to 12 ounces

Wick stickers (or hot glue, if you forget to order the wick stickers. I'm just saying . . . Also, tape works.)

Medium cotton wicks with wick tabs attached (can be purchased online or at your local craft store)

1 pound beeswax pellets or solid beeswax cut into small pieces

½ cup melted coconut oil

Continued

1. Prepare your containers by adding a wick sticker, dab of hot glue or piece of tape onto the bottom of each wick tab and press the tab firmly inside the bottom of each jar or tin.

2. Place the wax and coconut oil in a stainless-steel bowl. Set the bowl over a saucepan filled with 1 inch of boiling water over medium heat, stirring occasionally. (Alternatively, melt in a double boiler over low heat.)

3. When the mixture is completely melted, *carefully* pour the hot wax into the containers. Set the wicks so that they're centered, then lay a pencil or chopstick across the jars and tape the wicks to them.

4. Place the candles in a warm place, such as your oven (set it to WARM or 170°F while you're making the candles, then turn it off before placing the candles inside) to harden slowly. If they cool too quickly, the wax can crack.

5. Allow the candles to cure for 48 hours, then trim the wicks to about ¼ inch. Then, bask in the glow of DIY gone right.

UPCYCLED HONEY BEAR BOTTLE NIGHTLIGHT

The honey bear bottle: it's one of the best parts about eating honey, isn't it? Whenever I buy honey in a happy little bear-shaped bottle, I like to keep that bottle around for a long time—until there's literally nothing left in there, save for a few specks of crystallized honey. Over the years, I've discovered some pretty fun ways to reuse those cuties, such as adding a straw to make an ad hoc sippy cup for kids or turning them into liquid soap dispensers. Once, I even saw someone turn a massive collection of honey bears into a set of string lights. Blindingly cute! My personal favorite honey bear reuse, however, is this nightlight project. Quick, *so* simple to make and—because it's plastic and lit with an LED light—it's totally safe for any kid's room. It is seriously *the cutest*. So, next time you find yourself with an empty honey bottle shaped like a bear, don't toss it into the recycling bin. Instead, make this nightlight and get ready for some really sweet dreams.

Makes 1 nightlight

1 empty plastic honey bear bottle
White spray paint
Black permanent marker
Flameless LED tea light (color-changing, if desired)

1. Thoroughly wash the honey bear bottle inside and out, making sure to completely remove the label and any sticky residue.

2. Apply two thin layers of white spray paint to the outside of the bottle. Allow it to dry completely, then use the black marker to carefully redraw the bear's eyes and nose. (Just 3 small black dots will do the trick.)

3. Use the LED tea light to trace a circle on the bottom of the painted honey bear. Using a sharp craft knife, cut out the circle.

4. Push the tea light up into the hole, with the lightbulb pointing toward the bear's head. The fit should be tight. If you find that you've got some wiggling, you can secure the tea light with a bit of hot glue around the edge. And that's it! Good night.

PINECONE FIRE STARTER

Obsessed would be too strong a word to describe my husband's relationship with our fireplace, but only slightly so. Let's just say he has rarely turned down an opportunity to get a beautiful, crackling fire going—for popcorn popping, marshmallow toasting, or simply gazing upon. The guy is great at fire building and even better at keeping the fire going once it's started, but the starting can be tough. So much kindling. And paper. Starting and restarting. Thankfully, I discovered how to make these super-easy DIY fire starters that get our fires blazing in a flash (literally.) The finished product is so pretty you'll want to give them as hostess gifts in winter—just add a festive ribbon and a note. I even like to tote a couple along when we're invited to summer barbecues if I know the hosts have a firepit, since they're great for outdoor campfires, too. If you don't have an abundance of pinecones around where you live, you can order them online, pick them up at a craft supply store, or ask your local florist. To add color to your fire starters, drop in a couple of old crayons with the melting wax.

Makes 12 cones

1 pound beeswax pellets
Essential oil (optional)
12 dry pinecones
Glitter (optional)

Continued

1. Place the beeswax pellets in a stainless-steel bowl. Set the bowl over a saucepan filled with 1 inch of boiling water over medium heat, stirring occasionally. (Alternatively, melt in a double boiler over low heat.) Remove from the heat and add the essential oil, if using, stirring well to incorporate.

2. Using a pair of tongs, dip your pinecones in the wax mixture and set them aside on a waxed paper– or parchment paper–lined baking sheet to dry. Once dry to the touch, dip them again and allow them to dry on the lined pan. Repeat the process a third time to completely cover the pinecones in wax.

3. If decorating with glitter, lightly sprinkle the pinecone immediately after the last coating of wax is applied.

4. Allow the pinecones to dry for 2 hours, then store until ready to use.

Note: As with all flammable products, use extreme caution around pets or small children and keep fire starters out of their reach. Keep out of direct sunlight and away from direct heat sources.

ADDITIONAL RESOURCES

What to Do with the Dregs of Your Honey Pot

By this point, you're probably feeling that you've used honey in just about every imaginable way. You've slathered it on your face, squeezed it in your eyes, sipped it in a cocktail, and baked it in a cake. And now, sad as it may be, your honey pot hath runneth dry. Well, almost. See that layer of honey coating the bottom of the jar? It might be crystallized at this point, but it's definitely in there. That's still good, usable honey! Don't recycle the jar just yet. Here are five beyond-toast-or-tea uses for the remains of the day:

- Make the All-Purpose Sweet and Tangy Salad Dressing (page 83).
- Scrape it into a small bowl and serve it as part of a cheese plate.
- Drizzle it over roasted vegetables.
- Make a sweet and savory dip: Mix together 4 tablespoons of tahini or nut butter, 2 tablespoons of warm water, what's left of your honey, the juice of one lemon, a minced garlic clove, and a small handful of minced fresh mint. Season to taste with salt.
- Mix a cocktail—*right in the jar*! Stir in a tablespoon of hot water to make a syrup, then add a tablespoon of lemon juice,

an ounce of gin or bourbon, and a splash of seltzer. Grab a straw, and it's 5 o'clock. somewhere!

How to Substitute Honey for Sugar in Baking Recipes

You can substitute honey for sugar in most baking recipes with decidedly awesome results, but there's a catch: it's not an even trade. To make a successful swap, follow these simple rules:

1. Cut down on volume. Honey is much sweeter than sugar, so for every cup of sugar, substitute ½ to ⅔ cup of honey.

2. Reduce liquids. Honey is wet—made up of about 20 percent water—and sugar is, obviously, not. Therefore, you're going to need to adjust the total amount of liquid in a recipe to compensate for the extra moisture in honey. For every cup of honey you're using, subtract ¼ cup of other liquids from the recipe.

3. Lower the temperature. Honey burns faster than sugar. To be sure you're browning instead of burning, lower your oven temperature by 25°F and keep a close eye on whatever you're baking.

4. Add baking soda. Even if the recipe doesn't call for it. It helps balance the flavor and, because honey is acidic, it the baking soda–acid reaction offers a good rise. Add ¼ teaspoon of baking soda for every cup of honey in a recipe.

Growing a Bee-Friendly Garden

You don't have to become a beekeeper to do your part to help the ecosystem. Simply planting bee-friendly plants in your yard or garden will create a welcoming habitat for bees and may even help reverse the decline in their population! Follow these easy tips to add beauty and buzz to your surroundings:

Be a Grower, Not a Mower!

One of the easiest and most effective ways to make your yard more pollinator-friendly is to ditch the outdated notion of a manicured lawn; a sprawling expanse of grass is effectively a desert for bees. Even if you only carve out a small part of your property for flowering, pollen-producing plants, you're making a big difference for bees and other local pollinators. Such plants as dandelion, clover, chickweed, milkweed, and goldenrod—typically categorized as pesky weeds—are very important food sources for bees. Let them grow and flower in your yard! Consider your lawn a sort of a beautiful blooming meadow instead of a high-maintenance living carpet. Mow it less often, with your mower's height set a notch or two above the norm, and you'll create a much friendlier, much less bland-looking wildlife habitat.

Go Native and Go Easy

Bees love native wildflowers, flowering herbs, berries, and many flowering fruits and vegetables, so plant as many as you

can! A wide variety of locally indigenous flowers will boost pollinator efficiency and help a diverse species of pollinators thrive. Single flower tops, such as daisies and marigolds (as opposed to double-headed flowers, such as double impatiens, which contain extra petals that have replaced some or all of the reproductive parts of the flower), produce the most nectar and offer bees easy access to pollen. Flowers clustered into clumps of one type will attract more pollinators than individual plants scattered through your yard. Also, try to think about staggering plants that flower through spring, summer, and fall, so that you can support a range of bee species that fly at different times of the season. And—hopefully, it goes without saying— fungicides, herbicides, and pesticides are harmful to wildlife: bees, in particular, bring those substances back to their homes, sometimes with disastrous results. Please don't spray your garden with that stuff!

Provide Water

Make sure your garden includes a source of water for the bees. A birdbath, a little pond, even a fountain is a great way to offer bees the hydration they need to digest their food, and to regulate humidity and temperature back at the hive.

So, Like . . . What Exactly Should You Plant?

Bees have good color vision—they especially like blue, purple, white, and yellow blossoms. Studding your garden with those colors is an excellent starting point. Here is a short list of various plants that tend to attract a range of beneficial pollinators, but do some research to find out what's indigenous to your area and focus on those blooms.

FLOWERS

Cornflower

Cosmos

Daisy

Forget-me-not

Geranium

Marigold

Nasturtium

Poppy

Sunflower

FRUIT/VEGETABLES

Berries

Broccoli

Carrot

Cauliflower

Fennel

Stone fruit, all varieties

Yellow mustard

Zucchini

HERBS

Borage

Calendula

Catnip

Lavender

Lemon balm

Marshmallow

Rosemary

Sage

Thyme

A special note for apartment dwellers and other small space residents: Don't feel left out! Even if you only have room for a small planter or a window box, a few wildflowers or herbs, such as thyme and lavender, provide a nice foraging habitat for bees.

Becoming a Backyard Beekeeper

Can't get enough of that sweet, sweet honey and wondering whether you have what it takes to become a bona fide bee-keeper? There's a lot to contemplate when it comes to the business of bees. Here are three things to do and consider before you get started:

1. **Educate yourself.** There are many excellent books, organizations, and online resources about how to keep bees. But the best place to start is by getting to know other local beekeepers. They are perhaps your *most* valuable resource. Check out the local beekeeper directory on *Bee Culture Magazine*'s website to find experts near you (www.beeculture.com/directory).

2. **Assess your environment.** This may seem obvious, but you need to consider whether your foray into beekeeping will be welcome by those around you. Will your neighbors and family members be okay with your having bees around? Is anyone close to you allergic to bee stings? You also need to look into the legality of keeping bees where you live. Some municipalities prohibit backyard beekeeping. So, check on local laws before you zip up your bee suit. And if you live in a condo or apartment building, obviously, you'll need to check with your landlord or homeowners association before you take the plunge. After that, you'll need to make sure you have a hive location that gets both sun and shade and that has a source of water (which can be as simple as a birdbath) and access to flowering plants.

3. Think about the investment—time and money. Beekeeping isn't a "set it and forget it" kind of undertaking. To do it correctly and responsibly, you're going to need to make somewhat of a significant financial investment upfront (for your hive and all the necessary equipment) as well as a considerable investment of time on an ongoing basis. Expect to plunk down a minimum of several hundred dollars to get yourself set up, and plan on *at least* an hour of your time per hive per week. And know that, in all likelihood, you won't get honey your first year. It takes bees a long time to get going, so expect to have plenty of golden, flowing honey in year two.

4. Get all the right gear. You don't need *all* that much in the way of stuff to get going, but you do need more than just a bunch of bees. For starters, you'll need to get a hive, a bee veil and/or jacket, long leather gloves, a frame lifter, a bee brush, pliers, a smoker, and a hive tool. Many of these items are sold together in starter kits that are easily found online. Oh, and bees. You're going to need some. As tempting as it may be to buy your bees online like a new pair of shoes, it really isn't recommended. Instead, purchase them from a local backyard beekeeping enthusiast, someone who knows what he or she is doing, as the colony will already be accustomed to your area and you'll know something about the health of the hive.

5. Get a handle on bees. Knowing what you are getting yourself into and what it takes to keep a hive alive will be the key to your successful beekeeping.

ACKNOWLEDGMENTS

Many people were exceptionally generous to me while I was researching and writing *The Honey Companion*: sharing tips, information, recipes, and stories; helping to test (and taste) recipes and remedies; lending or recommending books and articles; teaching me about the amazing life of bees and letting me try all kinds of delicious honey.

Many thanks to Claire Marin and Tracy Gavant of Catskill Provisions for your abundance of ideas, time, and enthusiasm. And, mmmmm, that whiskey! You are a force to be reckoned with. And to Maggie Schwed, beekeeper (and walking encyclopedia) at Stone Barnes Center for Food and Agriculture, who gave me my first look at a real live beehive and answered all of my dumb questions with accessible clarity—thank you.

To my family, friends, and colleagues who enthusiastically and continually taste and test recipes with me and for me: I am grateful, as always, for your help and support. Sarah Blechman, I'm sorry you skinned your knee that day, but I appreciate your help with the book! (See? I promised!)

To my agent, Sharon Bowers, whose wisdom I cherish and whose support is endless, including at times when I refuse to remove the word "honey" from the subject line in a long chain of emails, because I find it both funny and endearing to have each message begin with that word: Honey, thank you.

Huge thanks to Ann Treistman, Aurora Bell, and the rest of the buzzing hive at The Countryman Press. I loved writing this book and am grateful to you for the opportunity to make it happen.

Of course, I couldn't have done any of this without the support, patience, and boundless love of my husband and our nutty little girls, who make all of it worth doing. I'm happy to be stuck with you. (Get it?)

CREDITS

INDEX